Palgrave Macmillan Studies in Family and Intimate Life

Titles include:

Graham Allan, Graham Crow and Sheila Hawker
STEPFAMILIES

Harriet Becher
FAMILY PRACTICES IN SOUTH ASIAN MUSLIM FAMILIES
Parenting in a Multi-Faith Britain

Elisa Rose Birch, Anh T. Le and Paul W. Miller
HOUSEHOLD DIVISIONS OF LABOUR
Teamwork, Gender and Time

Robbie Duschinsky and Leon Antonio Rocha (*editors*)
FOUCAULT, THE FAMILY AND POLITICS

Jacqui Gabb
RESEARCHING INTIMACY IN FAMILIES

Stephen Hicks
LESBIAN, GAY AND QUEER PARENTING
Families, Intimacies, Genealogies

Clare Holdsworth
FAMILY AND INTIMATE MOBILITIES

Peter Jackson (*editor*)
CHANGING FAMILIES, CHANGING FOOD

Riitta Jallinoja and Eric Widmer (*editors*)
FAMILIES AND KINSHIP IN CONTEMPORARY EUROPE
Rules and Practices of Relatedness

Lynn Jamieson, Ruth Lewis and Roona Simpson (*editors*)
RESEARCHING FAMILIES AND RELATIONSHIPS
Reflections on Process

David Morgan
RETHINKING FAMILY PRACTICES

Eriikka Oinonen
FAMILIES IN CONVERGING EUROPE
A Comparison of Forms, Structures and Ideals

Róisín Ryan-Flood
LESBIAN MOTHERHOOD
Gender, Families and Sexual Citizenship

Sally Sales
ADOPTION, FAMILY AND THE PARADOX OF ORIGINS
A Foucauldian History

Tam Sanger
TRANS PEOPLE'S PARTNERSHIPS
Towards an Ethics of Intimacy

Elizabeth B. Silva
TECHNOLOGY, CULTURE, FAMILY
Influences on Home Life

Lisa Smyth
THE DEMANDS OF MOTHERHOOD
Agents, Roles and Recognitions

Palgrave Macmillan Studies in Family and Intimate Life
Series Standing Order ISBN 978–0–230–51748–6 hardback
978–0–230–24924–0 paperback
(*outside North America only*)

You can receive future titles in this series as they are published by placing a standing order. Please contact your bookseller or, in case of difficulty, write to us at the address below with your name and address, the title of the series and the ISBN quoted above.

Customer Services Department, Macmillan Distribution Ltd, Houndmills, Basingstoke, Hampshire RG21 6XS, England

Family and Intimate Mobilities

Clare Holdsworth
Keele University, UK

palgrave
macmillan

First published 2013 by
PALGRAVE MACMILLAN

Palgrave Macmillan in the UK is an imprint of Macmillan Publishers Limited,
registered in England, company number 785998, of Houndmills, Basingstoke,
Hampshire RG21 6XS.

Palgrave Macmillan in the US is a division of St Martin's Press LLC,
175 Fifth Avenue, New York, NY 10010.

Palgrave Macmillan is the global academic imprint of the above companies
and has companies and representatives throughout the world.

Palgrave® and Macmillan® are registered trademarks in the United States,
the United Kingdom, Europe and other countries.

ISBN 978–0–230–59443–2

This book is printed on paper suitable for recycling and made from fully
managed and sustained forest sources. Logging, pulping and manufacturing
processes are expected to conform to the environmental regulations of the
country of origin.

A catalogue record for this book is available from the British Library.

A catalog record for this book is available from the Library of Congress.

10   9   8   7   6   5   4   3   2   1
22 21 20 19 18 17 16 15 14 13

Printed and bound in the United States of America

For Bethan, from whom I have learnt so much about coming to terms with family mobilities

Contents

Acknowledgements

This book was originally conceived in response to a request from David Morgan to contribute to the *Palgrave Macmillan Studies in Family and Intimate Life* series. David has continued to be the most generous and patient of editors and sustained and supported the writing of this book throughout, for which I am very grateful. I also collaborated with David on an earlier ESRC-funded project, 'The Transition out of the Parental Home in Britain, Spain and Norway', which I have returned to in the writing of this text. I was also encouraged to start writing this book by Bob Woods, who sadly passed away before its completion. Bob's commitment to writing and supporting more discursive contributions to population geography and medical history will be very greatly missed. In the course of writing this book I have benefitted from discussions about family and mobility with David Bissell, Bethan Evans, Bill Gould, David Featherstone, Sarah Hall, Denise Hinton, Helena Pimlott-Wilson, Jude Robinson, David Sadler, Johanna Waters, Ivo Wengraf and Paul Williamson. Many thanks also go to Sarah Hall for allowing me to reproduce data from her PhD research. I am also very grateful to the late Ray Pahl for permission to re-use material from the 'Managers and Their Wives' study which is held at the Qualidata Archive at the University of Essex. Pete Adey, Jacqui Gabb and Deirdre McKay very kindly read draft chapters, and I hope I have been able to do justice to their lively and thoughtful comments. I would also like to thank Beverley Sykes for her careful reading and correction of the manuscript and Andrew James at Palgrave Macmillan for his continual support.

Any study of family is always personal and this book is no exception. My family and friends, particularly Anne and David Becket, Janet Curran and John Hallett, have supported this project in so many ways and have helped me to make sense of the complexity, challenges and opportunities of family and intimate mobilities.

Series Editors' Preface

The remit of the *Palgrave Macmillan Studies in Family and Intimate Life* series is to publish major texts, monographs and edited collections focusing broadly on the sociological exploration of intimate relationships and family organisation. As editors we think such a series is timely. Expectations, commitments and practices have changed significantly in intimate relationships and family life in recent decades. This is very apparent in patterns of family formation and dissolution, demonstrated by trends in cohabitation, marriage and divorce. Changes in household living patterns over the last 20 years have also been marked, with more people living alone, adult children living longer in the parental home and more 'non-family' households being formed. Furthermore, there have been important shifts in the ways people construct intimate relationships. There are few comfortable certainties about the best ways of being a family man or woman, with once conventional gender roles no longer being widely accepted. The normative connection between sexual relationships and marriage or marriage-like relationships is also less powerful than it once was. Not only is greater sexual experimentation accepted, but it is now accepted at an earlier age. Moreover, heterosexuality is no longer the only mode of sexual relationship given legitimacy. In Britain, as elsewhere, gay male and lesbian partnerships are now socially and legally endorsed to a degree hardly imaginable in the mid-twentieth century. Increases in lone-parent families, the rapid growth of different types of stepfamily, the de-stigmatisation of births outside marriage and the rise in couples 'living-apart-together' (LATs) all provide further examples of the ways that 'being a couple', 'being a parent' and 'being a family' have diversified in recent years.

The fact that change in family life and intimate relationships has been so pervasive has resulted in renewed research interest from sociologists and other scholars. Increasing amounts of public funding have been directed to family research in recent years, in terms of both individual projects and the creation of family research centres of different hues. This research activity has been accompanied by the publication of some very important and influential books exploring different aspects of shifting family experience, in Britain and elsewhere. The *Palgrave Macmillan Studies in Family and Intimate Life* series hopes to add to this list of influential research-based texts, thereby contributing to existing knowledge and informing current debates. Our main audience consists of academics and advanced students, though we intend the books in the series to be accessible to a more general readership who wish to understand better the changing nature of contemporary family life and personal relationships.

We see the remit of the series as wide. The concept of 'family and intimate life' will be interpreted in a broad fashion. While the focus of the series will clearly be sociological, we take family and intimacy as being inclusive rather than exclusive. The series will cover a range of topics concerned with family practices and experiences, including, for example, partnership, marriage, parenting, domestic arrangements, kinship, demographic change, intergenerational ties, life course transitions, step-families, gay and lesbian relationships, lone-parent households and also non-familial intimate relationships such as friendships. We also wish to foster comparative research, as well as research on under-studied populations. The series will include different forms of books. Most will be theoretical or empirical monographs on particular substantive topics, though some may also have a strong methodological focus. In addition, we see edited collections as also falling within the series' remit, along with translations of significant publications in other languages. Finally, we intend the series to have an international appeal, in terms of both topics covered and authorship. Our goal is for the series to provide a forum for family sociologists conducting research in various societies, and not solely in Britain.

Graham Allan, Lynn Jamieson and David Morgan

1
Introduction

In 2012 a radio programme called *Ramblings* that aired on BBC Radio 4 featured presenters joining 'notable and interesting people on a walk through the countryside' (BBC, 2012). In one episode the presenter Clare Baldwin walked with Stuart and his dog Poppy, who were walking around England to raise money for charity and to raise awareness about mental-health issues. Clare and Stuart, along with Stuart's partner, discussed the benefits of walking for improving mental health and the simplicity of a life spent walking. Yet at one point in the conversation Stuart bemoaned that one of the problems of modern life is how we have less contact with family now than in the past. All three participants concurred with this observation, and most listeners probably took it as a statement of 'fact', similar to statements about the contraction of family connections that are frequently aired on radio and TV. However, given the context, I found the statement intriguing: the programme extolled the virtues of individual mobility and getting away from the trappings of modern life and consumerism while simultaneously identifying that it is because we spend so much time trying to get away from each other that modern life is so damaging. It is precisely this contradiction that has stimulated and sustained the writing of this book. In the course of writing I have become very alert to sweeping generalisations about the intensification of mobility at the expense of family that are very rarely challenged. In the week prior to the airing of the *Ramblings* programme, the United Kingdom's coalition government had announced plans to introduce a pilot scheme for universal parenting classes. Defending the intrusion of the state into family life, the TV presenter Katie Allsopp, in a debate on the BBC's *Newsnight* programme, had justified the need for state intervention on the premise that families do not live close to each other any more. According to Allsopp, whereas previous generations of mothers relied on the serendipity of living close to their mothers and aunts, present-day mothers are far more isolated. Putting aside for one moment the rather obvious counterclaim that mothers and daughters can stay in touch by using various forms of communication, this statement went unchallenged. Moving away from family members is one of the truths of modern family life. Different publics make the same interpretation of the relationship between family and mobility.

My point is that the assumption of universal dispersal does not stand up to closer inspection; it certainly holds for some individuals, but not all. Try explaining to residents of chawls in Mumbai, where generations of one family share a single domestic space, that the dominant experience of family life in the twenty-first century is isolation. For residents of expanding cities in both the global south and north, but particularly the south, the main pressure of modern living is overcrowding and the lack of opportunity for privacy and intimacy. In the global north a trend towards smaller households is evidenced, as an increasing number of households consist of only one resident. Yet the fragmentation of households does not automatically suggest dispersal. One of the flaws of the dispersal thesis is that it is not balanced and defies the fundamental assumption of Newtonian physics. We cannot all be moving away from each other, as at the same time this mobility will mean we are moving closer to others. I do not deny the intensification of mobility in late modernity, but this is not uniform; not moving away but growing up and staying in contact with friends and family remains a valid experience.

What is intriguing is that the assumption that family life has changed through mobility is rarely contested and is frequently alluded to in public commentary on social change. Yet such a straightforward and uncontested observation should be held up to closer academic scrutiny. In this book I explore both the evidence for the dispersal hypothesis and the possible reasons for its popularity. One possible explanation can be found in the dilemma briefly revealed in the *Ramblings* programme of the tension between individual and collective mobilities. If the benefits of individual mobility and freedom are emphasised, then this will have implications for more collective experiences. These different meanings of mobility and the tension between the self and more social forms are a quintessential part of family life. For example the main events of family life imply a different patterning of individual and collective mobilities: leaving home, getting married, having children and divorce and widowhood. Individual mobilities associated with these events will have implications for those either left behind or joined through mobility.

The study of mobility through key events can, though, reinforce a static or immobile reading of family, which is that if family is disrupted by mobility, this can result in the patterning of dispersal rather than in the revealing of the ongoing project of mobility in maintaining, sustaining and dissolving family. A more active and relational reading of family mobility corresponds to recent calls for a mobility turn in social sciences that has sought to challenge the amobile assumption of social-science enquiry. In seeking to invigorate this turn to the mobile, commentators point to the ubiquitous nature of myriad forms of mobility (spatial as well as social) and how mobility and movement are central to people's lives. The unique argument for this book is that a mobilities approach is pertinent to understanding family practices, and that while the tradition of approaching the family as a dynamic location of activities, rather than as a fixed and bounded group, is now well established in family sociology, the essence of movement intrinsic to family practices has received less attention. The mobilities turn does not just highlight the importance of mobility, but also shows how this movement is increasingly controlled and restricted. This is pertinent to thinking through family mobilities, specifically how these mobilities – on different spatial and temporal scales – are increasingly scrutinised, critiqued and regulated. Through developing synergies between the mobilities turn and family practices, my intention is to contribute to the mobilities approach, which has tended to prioritise the individual mobile body. My account will therefore foreground relational forms of mobility and think through how forms of connectedness are constructed, maintained and severed through mobile practices. The focus on family and intimate mobility developed in this book will provide a new perspective on mobilities that contrasts with more dominant individualised approaches.

The interplay between family practices and mobility can be usefully applied to the assumption of family decline through mobility. From this perspective there would appear to be transparent synergies between individualisation, mobility and family: the first two are essentially part of the same social processes which undermine the third. However, while not dismissing this normative portrayal of family as *anti*-mobility, a key argument throughout this book is that the oppositional approach to family and mobilities is too limiting and places too much emphasis on the social significance of propinquity and co-presence. As Urry (2007) suggests, families generate mobility and movement on different spatial and temporal scales. Examples of mobility practices that are generated through family practices include commuting, the school run, family visits and looking after relatives, travelling for/to family holidays and events as well as moving house, for example to be closer to 'good' schools, new jobs and employment opportunities and other family members.

The implicit assumption linking mobility and individualism against and ultimately counterpoised to family fails to consider the social significance of these mobile practices which are constantly reshaping and framing family and personal life. Distance (whether measured spatially or temporally) does not necessarily reduce the social and emotional significance of bonds between people, but can maintain these. The assumption that we are now living more individualised and isolated lives has been challenged by family sociologists recently; for example Carol Smart (2007) emphasises the importance of 'connectedness, relationality and embeddedness' and demonstrates empirically how these are essential themes in personal life. This book will extend this argument and will explore how these bonds between people are created, transformed and retained through movement and mobility. Family mobilities include a complex array of movements, some of which are chosen, deliberate and beneficial, while others are enacted out of obligation or force. Not all movements are necessarily observed or endorsed by significant others. Mobility can be associated with flight, running away from or intending to be with others. Movement can also be chaperoned or restricted. There is, therefore, more to family mobilities than the assumption that mobility and family are in opposition.

In bringing together recent contributions in family and mobility research, this book seeks to add to research in both domains, though the purpose is not to present a comprehensive account of the totality of family and intimate mobilities. Rather, my intention is to position family and intimate mobilities in relation to both theoretical accounts and empirical research. The context of empirical research is not defined: it can be present day, recent past or early modern, and the tension between continuity and change is a key theme for this book. Moreover, in bringing historical research on family mobility into this account I resists the overarching assumption that mobility is synonymous with modernity. This assumption does not hold for many of the practices to be considered here, such as leaving home, courtship and getting married. Empirically, the focus is predominantly western; this is not to dismiss the significance of mobility in the global south – quite the opposite, as to do justice to the variability of global mobility experiences falls outside the remit of this text. I use empirical studies from a number of different sources, including my own research and that of PhD students, as well as reanalysis of studies of family and community in the UK Data Archive, particularly Pahl's papers on his research on middle-class families in the 1960s. In order to present a more figurative portrayal of mobile bodies I also include discussions of characters and storylines in popular culture, including film and children's literature. It is a mixed bag of evidence, though the intention is not to be systematic but to think through a number of different positions on family mobility.

My account of family and intimate mobilities begins with a review of the mobilities turn, family practices and personal life in Chapter 2 in order to consider the multiple ways in which family mobility takes place. I explore how family and intimate mobilities can be used to decentre the family without reducing it to a loose gathering of atomised individual pathways. This reading also challenges the rather limited discussion of relationships in mobilities research, which is often dyadic rather than collective. Chapter 3 develops the theme of relationality, but from an individual perspective, by exploring how relationships are shaped through individual mobility. This account of intimate mobility uses a life course framework to unpack how relationships are formed, sustained and broken through mobility and how individual movement is both influenced by and impacts on others. Chapters 4 and 5 each consider collective forms of 'families on the move'. Chapter 4 focuses on more mainstream academic concerns: moving house and the intra-family movement associated with work and commuting. In bringing these two forms of mobilities together, I consider the relationship between mobility and immobility and how these sustain each other. Staying put and not moving, for example, may be achieved by the daily hypermobility associated with work, leisure and education. The account of collective mobilities is developed in Chapter 5 by using three further case studies of family mobility that return to the theme of decentring the family through a consideration of the child as a mobile subject; nomadic forms of family mobility, including family holidays; and non-linear mobilities between family and other 'near dwellers'. This chapter is set against grand narratives of social change through mobility, and the case studies are developed to refute the viewpoints that family life has broken down, that children are damaged through mobility or that no one stays in place any more. Chapter 6, which is the final, substantive chapter, reflects on what happens when mobility stops. In this chapter I outline the impossibility of mobility ever actually coming to an end and argue that closeness and belonging are experienced through mobility, rather than despite it. Finally in this chapter I outline how mobility can be denied. Not being able to move on and feeling trapped are not necessarily synonymous with belonging but with fear.

Throughout the text the opposition between the emancipatory potential of mobility and the fear of movement is a constant motif, and thus Cresswell's (2006) theorisation of nomadic and sedentarist metaphysics is apposite. Yet this binary distinction is heuristic; it is not a question of mobility being either 'good' or 'bad', but rather that mobilities in particular contexts and performed by different subjects will be interpreted somewhere within this dichotomy. The possibility of mobility producing both meanings is also valid. This returns us to the observations made by Stuart when walking with his dog Poppy that while his own personal mobility affords time and space away from others, he is also aware of the lack of conviviality due to geographical and temporal distance from others.

2
Theorising Mobilities and Family Practices

This chapter sets out a theoretical reading of family and intimate mobilities in which I review the main developments in both family practices and mobilities literature and draw out synergies between the two. The main aim is to explore how mobilities can be refashioned through an engagement with family practices and vice versa. The mobilities paradigm is, by nature, fluid and in constant development; and it is fitting with the philosophical bases of the mobilities turn that its relevance to other social science disciplines is explored. Moreover, this engagement should in turn generate re-visionist readings of mobilities.

At the centre of this re-visioning of both family practices and mobilities is the tension between family and relationality. That is, what is at issue is the extent to which we can assume that family has been replaced by a more individualised and reflective reading of personal relationships which emphasises subjective experiences rather than more collective affinities (Gilding, 2010; Ribbens McCarthy and Edwards, 2011). A focus on relationships rather than family is often dyadic and as such does not readily embrace the totality of affinities and intimate relations that are suggested by 'family'. There are other forms of relationships that pertain to a sense of being a 'social person' that are maybe less visible or tangible and might loosely be connected to a shared sense of family (Ribbens McCarthy, 2012). In recent years family researchers have sought to reassert the significance of family, which, while not inadvertently reproducing a functional interpretation of structure, can critically reclaim family 'as a central organising concept (alongside personal lives)... to address crucial personal, public and political dimensions' (Gillies, 2011: 10.1).

There are two important developments in family research, which I will discuss, that have sought to engage with the dialectic between the self and the social implied by family; these are family practices which focus on the 'doings' of family (Morgan, 2011) and personal lives (Smart, 2007), which prioritise the very different ways that bonds between people are maintained, sustained and broken. Both Smart and Morgan acknowledge commonalities in personal life and family practices, and I do not intend to unpick either the synergies or the contrasts between the two. Rather, for the purposes of developing a theoretical foundation for family mobilities, both approaches provide an alternative to writings about family that rely on structure and form but also resist the opposition between individual and collective affinities that can dominate accounts of individualisation. Moreover, as neither of these approaches is presented as a form of total theory, it is possible to utilise elements from both schemas. From family practices I take the relevance of the everyday as well as a distinction between habit and practice and the significance of practices being recognised and acknowledged by others. Following Morgan (2011), I will mostly restrict discussions to family or family-like relationships. Smart's (2007) account of personal life not only prioritises the complexity of personal affinities but also widens their scope over time and place.

Yet bringing mobilities into this dialogue between the self and the social can unsettle this relationship in a number of different ways. The mobilities literature has, to some extent, replicated the emphasis on individualised relationality. The need for mobilities to facilitate meeting up with other people is a key narrative (Urry, 2007), though this can emphasise individual connections rather than more social forms. We can imagine an individual agent moving around meeting other people, yet this does not necessarily capture the vitality and complexity of family mobilities as this vision continues to rely on the assumption of dialogic relationships and, moreover, of equality within networks. It also fails to consider interrelationships between others and relies on being able to draw the lines that link people together. The challenge from a mobilities perspective is to recognise both the complexity and the less tangible quality of intimate and family lives. Rather than replacing family with a more individualised notion of networks of relationships, what may be achieved here is a de-centring of family that recognises that mobilities are not just about the meeting of individual needs but can be brought about through relationships with others and are not always intended. In addition, the incorporation of the imaginary as well as physical connectivities can potentially extend the remit of family and intimate mobilities. Mobilities are also bound up with emotional control, facilitating how emotions within intimate relations are managed through spending time apart and together and maybe the fantasising about moving on or meeting up with as-yet-unknown others. The emotional dynamics of family life are driven by personal needs, but we also have to recognise those of others; for example, we might recognise the need to give someone 'space' in a relationship. Another limitation of a focus on individual relationships is that it may obscure power dimensions and inequalities within the family (Gilding, 2010). For some, the impossibility of mobility is a more pertinent issue than the freedom to move around to meet people. Exclusion from mobilities can be structural, reinforcing social, economic and cultural distinctions (Cass et al., 2005), and is shaped by gender and age relations within family settings.

Yet while mobilities can bring about a decentring of family, in other aspects a reading of family through a mobilities lens may also re-centre family. For example, the assumed tension between geographical mobility and family life is a long-standing interest in migration research (see, for example, Schneider and Collet, 2009; Schneider and Meil, 2008). Here the incompatibility between the self and the social is highlighted; we are not free to make individual mobility decisions as at times these are constrained by our relationships with others. This incompatibility is overstated, though, as mobility and migration can enable families and individuals to respond to changing and constraining circumstances. Jennifer Mason (2004a) usefully outlines a continuum of relationality, from more individualised forms to those that embrace inclusion and co-presence. Where there is consensus, a truce between fixidity and flow is possible, and this can be manifested through either collective mobility or immobility. For example, family holidays can be an expression of shared collective mobility, though they can also lead to discord and friction. In other contexts, individual relationality legitimises individual action in order to bring about benefits for others, and it is at these moments that family can be reconfigured through individual mobility. For example, offshore workers and long-distance drivers spend time away in order to financially support family members. In between these more extreme experiences, tensions between collective and individual forms will emerge that emphasise the incompatibility between individual (im)mobility and shared affinities. Given that many of us will experience relationality somewhere between these polarised states, in many instances this tension is resolved by a truce between the expectation of movement and the constraints on being mobile, which may be quite fleeting or negotiated over time. Hence a key consideration for an account of family and intimate mobilities is not just to focus on observed mobility practices but also to consider mobilities that are not realised yet continue to shape family relationships.

Thus mobilities can develop family and intimate lives in a number of different and, at times, contradictory ways. If it is possible to maintain a sense of family as existing between the social and the individual, then mobilities can reveal this less tangible and slippery notion of family, but we need to be alert to the very different ways in which mobilities create, sustain, modify and bring to close familial and intimate relations. In the next two sections, I outline how the main developments in family and mobilities theory can contribute to this endeavour, before concluding with a synergistic re-interpretation of these two approaches in order to extend the conceptualisation of family and intimate mobilities.

Families and intimacy

Family has sat uneasily in mainstream academic scholarship for many years. Even now, family is often linked with having children and 'family' as an adjective is often shorthand for intergenerational relations, particularly the relationship between parents and dependent children. So when we buy a family car, go on a family holiday or listen to politicians talking about 'hard-working families', we know who this 'family' refers to – parent(s) with dependent children. While nowadays we might be less concerned that there is only one parent or that parents are of the same sex, the emphasis remains that family is essentially taken to be referring to a dyadic union and their offspring. Thus a useful starting point for theorising family is Jon Bernardes' (1998) observation that the family does not exist. Writing in the 1990s in a textbook that sought to stimulate students' engagement with family studies, Bernardes acknowledges the difficulty of getting beyond symbolic and institutional readings of family. That this is problematic is not surprising, as there is no shortage of case studies demonstrating how the 'family' is held up as being responsible for so much of what is deemed wrong, as well as right, in modern industrialised societies. In the aftermath of the urban riots of August 2011 in the United Kingdom, many commentators were quick to blame the failure of the family for not disciplining children and therefore allowing the moral breakdown that erupted on the streets (Gillies, 2011). The readiness with which commentators made reference to the moral failure of the family reveals the dominance of normative evaluations of what the family should be and what it ought to do. Hence Bernardes' suggestions that in order to assist students who might be unfamiliar with the complexity of family and find it hard to see beyond its normative evaluations, the family needs to be stripped of its structural form. While the normative status of the family is continually held up by politicians, journalists and social commentators, among academic writers there has been equal engagement in attempting to dispel these myths. This is clearly an ongoing process; it is all too easy to lapse into a limited view of family that assumes a particular structure and a certain set of practices. Another way of expressing this is that as popular discourse simplifies the family, an important aim of social science enquiry is to challenge this oversimplification. If we do try to define 'the family', this very exercise might quickly reveal that while everyone knows what family is, there is no singular, cohesive meaning.

Individualisation

While the definition of family might be contested, there is greater convergence about the notion that family life in late modernity is undergoing profound changes, though the moral evaluation of these changes is more contested. A more populist interpretation is that the family is in decline and that this is related to the progression of individualisation, through which the centrality of the family is replaced by atomised, unconnected individuals. A more careful reading of individualisation, though, reveals that its main contributors make important distinctions in their evaluation of this process. According to Zygmunt Bauman's (2000) depiction of liquid modernity, we are living in a time when we are constantly faced with 'new' and distinctive problems that have to be continually encountered, and this is in contrast to more solid forms that were characterised by the certainty of structure and institutions. In contemporary societies the speeding up of social interactions that is endemic to late modernity means that these do not have time to coalesce in solid form. Thus without these certainties, institutions are in decline. In describing the anxieties that are brought about by living in a time of liquid modernity, Bauman portrays a world inhabited by people who are tied only to themselves and to their present. Yet not all interpretations of the changing family necessarily endorse the normative evaluation that Bauman predicts. Anthony Giddens (1992) in particular embraces a more optimistic reading of the transformation of intimacy and the possibility for individuals to embrace reflective and contingent relationships in late modernity. Identities are not fixed or given but are continually in development; thus we are all charged with maintaining 'do-it-yourself' biographies, and we cannot rely on the certainty of social structures or birth-right (see also Beck, 1992). Thus while Bauman expresses fear, Giddens seems to remove any emotion from his description of relationships. Consider, for example, his definition of a pure relationship as one that is

> entered into for its own sake, for what can be derived by each person from a sustained association with another; and which is continued only in so far as it is thought by both parties to deliver enough satisfactions for each individual to stay within it.
>
> (1992: 58)

For Giddens, the permeability of relationships is neither restrictive nor fearful, though it is rather anodyne. Yet what unifies Bauman's and Giddens' reading of the transformation of intimate life and social interactions is that these are predicated on movement; relationships are not fixed or tied to specific structural forms.

Family practices

The essential logic of individualisation is that family and intimacy are transformed through the processes of reflexivity. A limitation of this logic is that family becomes little more than a sum of its parts: a collection of permeable affinities. Yet the family can transcend individual relationships. So where does this leave the family? If it is not a structure and is not reduced to individualised affinities or identities, family remains a locale for collective activity arranged over varied spatial and temporal configurations. Family is therefore, as David Morgan (2011) suggests, more properly used as a verb, rather than as a noun or an adjective. Morgan's use of family practices develops six main themes that are implied by the term practice: linking the perspectives of the observer and the actor; a sense of the active; a sense of the everyday; a sense of the regular; a sense of fluidity; and a linking of history and biography. Moreover, as Morgan suggests, these headline themes cannot be divisible, in that they have to be taken as influencing each other. In other words, the significance of family practices is that they are often unremarkable, as family is just 'done'. This morphs into a sense of family as active, fluid and almost banal: family practices can in some instances be taken as too trivial to be commented on or distinguished from other events. Morgan argues that family is not to be distinguished by its absence (that is, that family is in decline), but rather that family practices are continually in the process of (re-)creation.

Morgan argues for a fuzziness about family life that contrasts with the expectation that family should take a specific form. He also recognises, however, that family is not repeatedly started from scratch; we are not continually having to reinvent practices, but rather these are shaped by 'legal prescriptions, economic constraints and cultural definition' (Ibid.: 7). Family practices not only are visible to and recognised by those in the family but are also celebrated and endorsed by others. The importance of displays of family practices reveals the importance of the quality of familial relationships and that these need to be renewed. It is not sufficient simply to acknowledge the existence of relationships, as these need to be reaffirmed (Finch, 2007). Morgan's use of practices incorporates Bourdieu's reading of practice and structuration, which maintains an emphasis on sets of processes rather than 'fixed external structures' (Morgan, 2011: 7). For Bourdieu, the family is both immanent in individuals *and* transcendent – that is, the family is rooted in the objectivity of social structures and the 'subjectivity of objectively orchestrated mental structures' (Bourdieu, 1996: 21). Thus family is therefore both fixed and external: it appears to us with the opacity and solidity of a thing, but it is also the product of acts of social production. Bourdieu therefore resists the interpretation of the family that is predominant in lay discourses, as 'active agent, endowed with a will, capable of thought, feeling and action' (Bourdieu, 1998: 65). Yet, at the same time, this practice approach retains a sense of the family as more than a space or entity for housing intimate relations. It is precisely this reading of the family as both structural and fluid that can be usefully developed from a mobilities perspective, as it can move the study of mobilities from a focus on individual connectivities to a consideration of the relational aspects of mobility.

For Bourdieu, however, the family is also a key site of social repro-duction and 'plays a decisive role in the reproduction of the social order' (Bourdieu, 1996: 23). This approach has been developed, par-ticularly in sociology of education, where the family is often taken as an incubator of habitus. Habitus is a key concept in Bourdieu's the-ory of practice, and it is defined as 'a durable, transposable system of definitions acquired initially by the young child in the home as a result of the conscious and unconscious practices of her/his family' (Bourdieu, 1992: 134). Yet while this reading of the role of family in social reproduction has a certain empirical and ideological neatness, the idea that the family is an important locale for socialisation and the acquisition of conscious and unconscious practices may result in a fixed and objective reading of family. That is, if the family is taken as a locale for socialisation, then family becomes a 'thing' and a generator of practice (see, for example, Atkinson, 2011).

For my purposes, the significance of the immanent and transcen-dent properties of family alerts us to the pitfalls of both normative and structural readings of family and, in particular, to the fact that we need to be wary of the black box metaphor. Family cannot be treated as a structure within which practices are fashioned, and family does not have active agency over and above that of its members. Thus, as Morgan remarks, there is an ongoing tension between agency and structure that cannot be easily resolved. A further observation about practice is that it can never be reduced to a set of individual acts: we might be considering the habits or behaviour of an individual, but these dispositions are unconsciously reproduced as well as shared and known by others.

It is also important to resolve intentions and reflectivity in fam-ily practices, which is a key theme in Morgan's theory of family practices. On the one hand he rejects the importance of structure and form, but on the other, in opposition to Bauman and Giddens, he recognises the importance of the trivial and habitual qualities of doing family. Thus in Giddens' (1992) reading of the reflective self, individuals are repeatedly reassessing their options, working out what they get out of relationships and balancing different options and choices. Morgan resists this assumption that we are endlessly reflective; there are, he argues, many instances where practices cannot be reduced to individual rationality and decision making. The family practices approach is not, therefore, so much a refutation of individualisation, but rather resists some of its logic; in particular, it retains the relationality of family rather than the more egocentric assumption of individualisation. It also resists the need to document and clarify the direction of change in family life; instead, it prioritises diversity and, in particular, variations in practices over the life course.

Personal life

There are other important developments in family theorisation that are relevant in developing the concept of family practices, particularly recent writings on personal life. The idea of personal life is that it seeks to overcome the distinction between public and private in locating the personal, both within and between these spaces. What is more, as Carol Smart has proposed, the development of personal life is not restricted to family but rather seeks to bring together different kinds of kinship and family relationships with friendships. Smart's approach is also engaged in going beyond a materialist reading of practice, in that family matters not just in terms what members do but also in terms of how families and relationships 'exist in our imaginations and memories, since these are just as real' (2007: 4).

There are a number of key tenets of personal life that overlap to some extent with the practices approach. It resists the inevitable conclusions of the individualisation thesis that have dominated certain aspects of academic scholarship and popular discourses on family, particularly the idea that there is a growing tension between individual agency and relational affinities. Rather, Smart argues that it is necessary to distinguish the personal from the individual; while the latter prioritises reflexivity, the personal emphasises relationality, as a sense of self and personhood is developed *through* relationships with others. In developing the theme of personal life, Smart argues that the morally grounded and relational concept of a 'life project' is more empirically accurate in capturing the complexity of contemporary familial and non-familial relationships than the more narcissistic idea of the do-it-yourself biography.

Smart's emphasis on movement and imagination is important to consider, and again it is in contrast to the main assumptions of individualisation. In particular, in Giddens' formulation, the reflective self is able to leave relationships behind, and the ephemeral quality of confluent love is possible because of the expectation that people will, and can, move on. Yet for Smart, personal life does not evolve around a series of encounters; rather, life projects become more complex and intertwined as relationships form and maybe dissolve. This approach is developed in her seminal empirical research on divorce and co-parenting, carried out in collaboration with Bren Neale (1999). They illustrate how relationships are not brought to an abrupt end through divorce and how parenting has to be refashioned after separation. Parents have to reassess their roles and responsibilities as mothers and fathers and their relationships to each other and their children. The complexity of family life can therefore be intensified by the processes of relationship formation and breakdown.

The significance of memory and biography also resists Bauman's depiction of late modernity in which people are only attached to the present. A key theme that Smart explores is how personal life is in constant motion. This emphasis on fluidity is relevant for realised changes in relationships, but also in the ongoing process of revisiting relationships, both in the recent past and in the imagination. Smart, for example, considers the popularity of family genealogy and how the process of revealing 'true selves' through family heritage is a way of solidifying these imaginary relationships. Pouring over the life histories of people who we have never known and who lived in times that might be very alien to our own gives us a sense of self-identity that transcends the present.

Intimacy and emotion

Both Morgan and Smart acknowledge the contribution of scholarship on intimacy in moving beyond normative and institutional interpretations of family. For example, Lynn Jamieson's (1998) analysis of the significance of intimacy in personal life makes the case for a more grounded approach to disclosing intimacy that acknowledges how personal relationships are dependent as much on mutual support as they are on intense ways of disclosing intimacy. Hence the sociological turn to considering intimacy and emotions and the move away from more traditional concerns with structures and institutions do not infer that we should reify the individual (and his/her emotional attachment to others), as the study of intimacy does not preclude socio-cultural perspectives. In other words, a shift of focus from family to intimacy does not necessarily imply a preoccupation with individual subjectivities.

The traditional dichotomy between rational, purposeful action and emotional, non-rational acts has dominated the development of social sciences, yet the validity of this dichotomy has been challenged through the cultural turn, which has resisted the polarisation between rational and emotional through consideration of the embodied subject. Deborah Lupton (1998) writes about the emotional self as a socio-cultural exploration; while acknowledging the 'slipperiness' of the concept of emotions, she seeks to expound how experiences of emotions are produced by embodied subjects. She contrasts a popular or inherent approach to emotions with an interpretation of emotions that is framed by socio-cultural norms. From the latter perspective, emotions remain a perpetually shifting target, yet how we make sense of these emotions is not only part of the 'project of subjectivity' but also reflects how individuals are acculturated into particular socio-cultural contexts. The importance of acculturation, though, does not mean that the emotional self is fixed, as Lupton writes:

> [t]he emotional self is dynamic, responsive to changes in socio-cultural meanings and representation and in individuals' own biographies of interactions with others as well as with inanimate things (such as place and objects).
>
> (1998: 168)

Emotions are therefore central to untangling the dialectic between the self and the social. In her account of the 'sociality of emotions', Sara Ahmed (2004: 10) argues that 'emotions create the very effect of the surfaces and boundaries that allow us to distinguish an inside and an outside in the first place'. In other words, emotions are neither in the self nor do they emanate from 'out there', but they form the boundaries that register the proximity of others. A focus on emotions does not, therefore, mean a concern with these individual experiences but rather emphasises 'social presence' (Ibid.: 10).

This idea of the social presence of emotions alerts us to the 'intimate contours of our lives' (Ibid.: 202) and the importance of time. We carry the traces of our past lives with us, and our emotions shape interactions with others as well as anticipate what might come. Yet there is also unevenness to the sociality of emotions. The emotional management that we need to do as part of the project of the self is highly varied. In some contexts it is barely conscious and just part of daily routines and strategies, yet at other times we are very much aware of the need to deal with difficult emotional experiences and how these are brought about through interactions with others. This awareness of the variability of emotions and the ongoing process of emotional management develops the family practices/personal lives approach. It alerts us to the possibility that there is an emotional unevenness to practices, ranging from the routine and semi-conscious to more challenging behaviours and situations. Thus we might anticipate that mobility is inherent to disclosing intimacy and emotion within families and relationships. Moreover, emotions are also fluid and mobile. In recent geographical entanglings with emotion and affect, a shared ontology of emotion that most commentators would recognise is a relational one; what is of interest is the flow of emotions and affect between people and objects (Pile, 2010). Yet this ontology also 'privileges proximity and intimacy' (Ibid.: 10) and an empirical drive to disclose intimacy and closeness.

To summarise, following recent conceptualisations of family practices and personal life, particularly by Morgan and Smart, the theoretical approach to family that I develop here does not rely on an undiluted reading of individualisation. This is not to undermine some of the profound changes that are bringing about a reinvention of family life, but rather to demonstrate that the essence of family continues to evolve around affinities and relationality rather than the individual; it is this sense of collectivity that can provide a fulcrum for theorising family and intimate mobilities.

Mobilities

Analogous to the ways in which the family practices approach focuses on the continual relevance of family as a meaningful entity that cannot be reduced to individual agency, the mobilities turn not just directs towards documenting movement but considers how this movement is central to most people's lives. In addition, a focus on mobility implies relationality and forming connections, and maintaining these as well as dissolving them. We cannot think about relationships without recognising how these are shaped by mobility, from moving in, to moving forward and moving out, so it is reasonable to assume that the opposite should also be true – that we cannot think about mobility without thinking about relationships.

The mobilities turn is a new, ongoing, interdisciplinary paradigm in social sciences; it is not just concerned with re-theorising mobility and movement, but, more radically, concerns a re-visioning of the social *through* mobility rather than stasis and structure (Sheller and Urry, 2006). A useful way, though, of approaching this paradigm is by considering the magnitude and significance of mobility. Data on the quantity of mobility in its myriad forms, for example from the number of passengers embarking on car journeys, bus trips, rail journeys or flights to the number of displaced persons, asylum seekers and migrant workers, offer a snapshot of the sheer force and magnitude of human mobility. This lends itself readily to a discussion of the significance of mobility. Peter Adey (2010), for example, begins his text on mobilities with a brief discussion of his daily commute to work and the complexity and variability of mobilities that this involves. Discussions of mobility are not restricted to corporeal forms but also incorporate the movements of goods, services and information. Yet while headline data on the magnitude of mobilities is an appealing way of making the case for mobility as a fulcrum of social science research, the more substantial rationale of the mobilities turn is that without mobilities, society does not exist. This repositioning of social science enquiry is most closely associated with a number of key contributors, particular John Urry (2000, 2007).

The mobilities turn

Urry's starting point is that social science has been fixated by immobility and structures, and it needs re-imagination to acknowledge the social through complex mobilities. Yet this focus on mobilities also involves an understanding of how complex mobilities are sustained by immobilities or moorings. These include facilities and infrastructure as well as technologies, from roads and railways to cars and mobile phones. The fixidity of these objects is not necessarily permanent, but may involve temporary storage or lack of use. An important aim of the mobilities turn is not, therefore, to focus exclusively on movement but rather to explore the relationship between mobility and immobility. This tension between mobility and immobility is not just related to infrastructure and objects but also to the dynamic interplay between them. Moreover, mobilities do not necessarily displace or replace immobility; there is 'no linear increase in fluidity without extensive systems of immobility' (Urry, 2007: 54). This interplay is particularly relevant for family and intimate mobilities, and one of the key themes to develop is the interplay between individual patterns of mobility and immobility: how some mobility practices are sustained by the immobility of others and the intensification of mobilities for some is brought about through the immobilisation of others.

Conceptually, this seamless boundary between mobility and immobility can be difficult to visualise and document. As Adey (2006) warns, if everything becomes mobile, then mobility itself means nothing. The extent of the relationality between different mobilities and immobilites is theoretically extensive, yet the density of interconnections also renders these invisible, so much so that they are often only revealed when mobilities are suspended. Freak weather conditions provide an intriguing example of how the intricacies of connections become visible though failure. For example, during most winters in the United Kingdom, extensive snowfall will bring about travel disruption for a few days; people's everyday mobilities are impeded, and this often leads to the closure of schools as teachers cannot travel to work. This in turn means that parents have to take time off work and rely on others to cover for them; some of these parents will be teachers, who will be faced with the dilemma of either trying to get to work or looking after their own children. The official advice at these times is that we should only embark on 'essential' journeys, though the distinction between what is essential and what is not is far from transparent. Essential does include commitments to others, so it is reasonable to assume that hospital personnel getting to work are embarking on 'essential journeys', yet does not include visiting friends and family, even though the latter mobilities may also be essential for the provision of care. The dilemma facing teachers and other employees in similar occupations is that the mobilities that are essential in order to fulfil commitments to keep services open for others are impeded by other responsibilities and our interdependencies with others, both known and unknown.

Our response to these moments of suspension is usually very personal. We are aware of our own inconvenience and are often very quick to blame others. Disruption can also engender anxiety about mobilities, as what are normally taken-for-granted journeys become challenging and uncertain. Media coverage of school closures is often very critical of teachers' inability to travel to work, claiming that it is unreasonable to expect other workers to take a day off work to look after their children. But this moment of suspension, while revealing the intensity of the relationality of (im)mobilities, is not interpreted in this way; it appears that we are more frustrated by our dependency on others and still hold to the ideal that mobility is a manifestation of independence. Moreover, the fact that teachers struggle to get to work because their journeys are often not on the public transport links or road networks that are prioritised to be kept open during bad weather is rarely discussed. Thus, snow disruption also reveals the assumed priorities of mobilities, which are that movements associated with economic activity are prioritised over other forms: major transport links between business districts and those essential for the movement of goods are kept open, while routes to schools, which are often outside business districts, are not. The complexity of mobilities that is revealed by extreme weather conditions therefore also exposes how the provision of transport technologies results in a gender bias for users with respect to frequency, distance and form (Law, 1999; Uteng and Cresswell, 2008). Mobility technologies that are not primarily directed towards facilitating commuting and the transportation of goods and financial services are more likely to be localised and slower. Mobilities that are primarily associated with sustaining family life, and thus are more likely to be used by women, do not necessarily benefit from the same level of infrastructure improvements that are legitimised for large-scale projects, such as high-speed rail networks, on the basis of their potential contribution to economic growth.

Networks and meetings

The pattern of mobilities revealed by snow disruption would appear to be representative of a network of interconnected mobilities and that we are now living in what Manuel Castells (1996) has coined a networked society. The significance of networks for Castells is that unlike structures, which imply a centre or hierarchy, the network society is 'characterised by the pre-eminence of the social morphology over social action' (quoted in Urry, 2007: 212). The problem with snow is that everything comes to a halt because all connections are dependent on each other, rather than being fixed to one particular point.

For Urry, the rise of networks is also associated with an opening up of family life. The geographical dispersal of family and friends means that we cannot rely on the serendipity of propinquity; that is, we can no longer depend on frequent and chance encounters to maintain intimate and family relations, but rather we have to plan encounters. As Urry writes, 'planned meetings are central to many people's lives and this seems true of many kinds of networks' (2007: 220). Encounters are increasingly fleeting and ephemeral; we may know a lot of people, but not necessarily very well. We are, as Granovetter (1973) famously argued, dependent on the 'strength of weak ties'. In the networked society there is also a blur between public and private, as networks of family, friends and colleagues intertwine and cross over (see also Wittel, 2001).

Yet while networks might reveal how personal life is organised, this emphasis on planning and knowing also impacts the quality and emotionality of relationships. Elliott and Urry describe how the complexity of contemporary mobilities not only layers the ordering of space, place and time but also 'drains the emotional energies of women and men' (2010: 96). Therefore the significance of mobile lives is not restricted to movement but is bound up with the project of self-development and personhood. The reflective self of late-modernity is also a mobile self, and this mobility is corporeal, imaginative and developmental. We do not stay still, not just physically, but in terms of our own identities, relationships, and desires and aspirations. Thus the transformation of intimacy that characterises late modernity is intricately bound up with mobilities, and there is a theoretical neatness to the fusion of the mobilities paradigm and the individualised self, with the two inferring each other. Herein, though, lies the theoretical challenge of developing the study of family and intimate mobilities, which is to resist the emphasis on the individual actor as opposed to more collective and interdependent mobilities. Furthermore, this interdependency does not necessarily prioritise moving together and co-presence, but it also involves moving apart as well as illicit or forced mobilities. I will consider the implications of the family practices thesis for mobilities in the last section of this chapter, but before doing so it is important to consider the meanings of mobility because we do not just 'do' mobility. Movement itself is transformatory, changing more than just our relationships with others; it changes our own identities and sense of mobile 'personhood' too.

Meanings and emotional forms of mobilities

The observation that contemporary society depends on mobility could be interpreted as instrumental. Yet the mobilities turn is not just restricted to institutional forms of movement but also seeks to interrogate mobility through a socio-cultural lens. The claim that mobility matters is as important as documenting the magnitude of mobility. Tim Cresswell's (2006) writings in particular have developed a way of revealing the cultural significance of mobility. Cresswell draws a distinction between mobility and movement – that mobility is movement plus meaning. His description is analogous to how physicists might regard speed as an outcome of distance and time. This use of formulaic representation seeks to underscore the importance of his observation. Mobility is life itself – it is more than getting from A to B; it is what happens when getting from A to B that matters. From this viewpoint it is not how mobility brings people together or pushes them apart that matters, but what is revealed through the very act of mobility that should be prioritised.

Yet Creswell's interpretation of what is meaningful about mobilities is also very loose, and emotions are experienced, made sense of and managed through mobility in a variety of different ways. Mobility can facilitate emotions by creating opportunities for co-presence as well as separation; it can be a form of emotional control (the need to get out of certain situations or the need to feel closer), but it also opens up the unknown and unfamiliar, engendering a sense of emotional uncertainly that renders the unconscious maintenance of emotions impossible. Mobility allows for expression of emotional forms that are destabilising, as in Lupton's (1998) description of the appeal of carnivalesque experiences as a way of relaxing the social norms and the need to controls one's emotions that are constantly sought in contemporary industrialised societies. The desire to 'get away from it all', to travel, meet new people and experience new settings is a popular motif. Yet mobility does not just allow for the relaxation of emotional control; it also allows for emotions within intimate relations to be managed: spending time apart and spending time together. More sinister emotional control can be forced on others, either through denying mobility or through enforced expulsion. Feelings of entrapment and the inability to escape from oppressive relationships are just as relevant to the interplay between emotion, intimacy and mobility as more celebrated forms.

In acknowledging this darker side to mobilities, we can see that the meanings ascribed to movement may be quite polarised. Cresswell usefully develops a heuristic dichotomy between two opposing metaphysics of mobility: nomadic and sedentarist, both of which can be seen to apply to family and intimate forms. The sedentarist reading is a more popular interpretation of family mobility and assumes that mobility is a threat to family. In the sedentarist schema mobility threatens; it underlines the distinction between stranger and familiar and reveals those who live on the outside of society. As the family is popularly located as an essential social form, this threatening character of mobility is particularly pernicious to family. Thus we have to work hard to maintain family, despite mobility. In opposition to this perspective, the nomadic metaphysics emphasises the potentiality of mobility. It is maybe more individualistic on first reading, as the expressive form of mobility associated with the nomadic very much promotes the ideal of individual freedom, though we can interpret this freedom in different ways. It is useful to adapt Berlin's (2002) distinction between positive freedom (freedom to) and negative freedom (freedom from): freedom from might imply a more individualistic movement away from family and kin, but freedom to implies a more relational form, such as the freedom to develop relationships of choice. The nomadic metaphysics conjures up the importance of individual mobility in framing family practices: moving on and moving in are celebrations of key moments of family life that are created through mobility. From leaving home and coming out (which has a number of different meanings in itself) to moving in and 'going away', and so on, many of the celebrated moments in intimacy and family life imply mobility. Nomadic expressions of mobility can also be experienced collectively, from the great mobilisations of people due to repression – political, economic or cultural – to the popularity of festivals and collective tourist mobilities (for example, the hedonistic culture popularised on the Spanish Balearic Islands); the freedom of expression through mobility can be shared with others. Collective mobilities that engender the possibility of positive freedom may therefore be facilitated by mobilities events, such as festivals or rallies, that bring people together.

Nomadic and sedentarist metaphysics provide a valuable framework for recognising the plurality of meanings ascribed to family mobility. In particular, it is all too easy to bemoan how family is undermined through mobility and ignore how more expressive forms of mobility are equally valid. This tension between sedentarist and nomadic metaphysics is interwoven into family practices and varies over the life course. We might anticipate, for example, a very different interpretation of long-distance mobility for young people at a time of transition compared with that of partners in commuter marriages. How mobility is interpreted is not, therefore, just an individual process but is very much shaped by the interdependencies and connectivities that are produced through mobility.

Mobilities over time

Time is an important constituent of the mobilities turn, as both speed and magnitude of mobility are constantly shifting. The mobilities turn is not just about making the case for changing the magnitude and significance of mobility but also points to the increasing pace and intensity of mobility that are profound for social structures. An important component of the mobilities turn is that individuals are more mobile. Not only people but also objects and resources can all be moved around quicker and across boundaries; sometimes this is not dependent on actual moment, but can be done by proxies. It is relatively straightforward to extrapolate from the increased pace of mobilities that changes in family life and the heightened fluidity and speed in contemporary life are popularly recognised as causal factors in bringing about family change. Yet while the forms of mobility that have developed during the twentieth century have radically altered how mobility is experienced with reference to distance and time, the contribution of mobility to family practices, particularly the formation and dissolution of relationships, is more constant. Leslie Page Moch's (2003) account of moving Europeans from 1650 to the present time considers how mobility and migration have enabled families and individuals to respond to changing circumstances. Young people in particular have always left home to seek out new opportunities in employment and relationships, often out of necessity rather than choice, while marriage has traditionally been celebrated or made possible by mobilities, for example couples might elope, while women are 'given away' and carried over the 'threshold' of a new home. Thus some of the mobilities that are part of family practices are not 'new' but rather are found in most systems of family and household formation. Movement has always been a prerequisite for relationship formation as well as a way of adapting to change. Moreover, mobilities are not always rooted in the present but are both anticipated and remembered, and, to develop John Gillis' (1996) account of myth and ritual in family life, the mobilities we live by can be as formative as those we live with. Rather than emphasising social change, it is reasonable to assume that family mobility embraces continuity and change, integrating new forms of mobility as well as being shaped by institutional and cultural meanings.

Family and intimate mobilities

The discussion of mobilities so far has attempted to consider the relevance of the mobilities paradigm to family and intimate life, and mobility scholars have certainly not ignored the significance of this re-visioning of dialectic between the self and the social for family and intimate relations. To date this has mostly been achieved by focussing on 'new' forms of intimacy, such as living-apart-together (LAT) couples, commuter marriages and transnational families, and how these are created and sustained by mobility practices. Thus a key tenet of the mobilities paradigm is that increased mobility is not just about more individuals moving around doing their own thing, but it is also about enabling people to be together. As the capacity for staying in touch and 'being there' is enhanced by diverse technologies, it creates a networked society of individuals that is certainly not individualised (Urry, 2007). While patterns of residence might suggest a shift towards more atomised forms of living, as evidenced by the increase of one-person households in most advanced economies in recent years, this is balanced by a sense of 'meetingness'. This, as Urry (2003) defines it, refers to the ongoing co-ordination of social gatherings, when we can be with friends and family as well as work colleagues and business partners or more casual acquaintances. Increasingly, the seemingly incompatible trends towards both more individualised ways of living and an increase in the urge to travel to spend time with others are refashioning intimate relations and creating a more complex spatial geometry of intimacy.

However, while the emergence of new forms of intimacy is certainly worthy of note, I suggest that it is possible to be more ambitious in mapping out the potentiality of family and intimate mobilities. There are numerous different ways in which this can be approached, and potentially anything is up for grabs here, as any configuration of intimate relations is 'familial', and a move away from a fixed residence means that family membership is also fluid and changing. A dynamic family is one that is not only spatially diverse but also looks to the past and future.

A useful starting point here is Tom Cooke's (2008) claim, in his paper on family migration, that 'all migration is family migration'. Cooke's argument is that while geographers have identified the significance of family migration when this involves family members moving together, 'family' is also inferred in seemingly individual migration practices. The decision to move, or not to move, to a chosen destination and the possibility of return are made with reference to others. Cooke's review of the development of 'family migration literature' traces the emergence of a life course perspective in family migration research that has sought to reveal the complexity of family mobility and to challenge more traditional human capital theorisations of individual migration. Thus Cooke argues that the future possibilities for research on family migration are potentially endless, as all forms of migration should be treated as 'family' migration.

Can the same argument be made for 'mobility'? Clearly, the distinction between mobility and migration is relevant here. Migration focuses on clearly delimited movement in time and space and foregrounds a more purposeful movement between a fixed point of origin and destination, in contrast with the variability of mobilities. A more plausible claim could be that all mobility is relational, and in many ways, as outlined above, the mobilities paradigm has embraced this. But to date, mobilities literature has not really taken this argument to its full potential or conclusion. The main conceptual barrier that exists between recent theoretical developments of family practices and mobility is that the former has increasingly sought to lay bare the centrality of the individual and replace it with a more relational emphasis on the personal and the significance of shared experiences and practices. The mobilities literature certainly engages with the idea of relationality in recognising that we need to move to be with other people and also need to be with other people when we move. One of Urry's key questions is why do we still travel, given that technology can do so much of our mobilities for us? Technology allows us to communicate, engage in imagined mobility and consume, and so on, but despite, or maybe because of this, the basic premise of corporeal mobility remains meeting people. Physical co-presence matters. Yet this falls short of the real value of mobilities to family and intimacy. The limitation of a network or meetings approach is that it remains egocentric, and so the focus is on relationships between one person and others rather than on the complexity of relational affinities, not all of which are experienced equally. Additionally, so much of family mobility is unseen. This is, I think, the value of Cooke's claim that all migration is family migration. Cooke's argument is rooted in a very different literature – that of population geography. As population geographers became interested in the complexity of family migration in the 1990s, the implications of this enquiry were quickly revealed, particularly how individual migration decisions impacted others. The household did not move as one, because the outcomes of migration on household members varied. Family mobilities should not, therefore, just focus on how people are brought together through movement, or on identifying new and visible ways of sustaining relationships, but should also consider how mobilities and immobilities are intertwined.

Thus family and intimate mobilities can be extended beyond meetings and networks to consider more varied forms of moving together and apart, alone or together, such as the following:

• Mobility is about moving away from others in addition to co-presence. It can be about leaving others behind, and it can bring about the end of relationships as well as the formation of new ones and the continuation of existing ones. Social connections can be extended to include the traces of mobilities that we leave behind and those which we take with us. Thus, intimate mobilities are both multidirectional and continual, and the emotional dynamics of relationships are driven by the possibility of both moving on and returning.

- This incessant sense of movement can be collective and individual as well as temporary or permanent. For example, family holidays offer an opportunity for escape and a collective suspension of everyday mobilities and practices. But holidays are framed by departure and return: they are planned, anticipated and looked forward to, yet the experience of being away is balanced by the expectation of returning and indeed the need to return.

- Mobility is not necessarily an act of choice, and the degree to which the mobile subject is autonomous will vary greatly. Consider the teenager kicked out of the family home, the trafficked woman forced into marriage with a stranger, or family visits embarked on out of obligation. These relational mobilities are not necessarily chosen but may be forced, be embarked on out of a sense of duty or in order to be able to care for others.

- Mobility does not necessarily imply destination, yet how this is evaluated varies over the life course. Compare, for example, the affirmative endorsement of youthful wanderlust with the institutional containment of wanderings of elderly dementia patients. Youth is afforded the privilege of wandering with the expectation that these liminal wanderings will end in stasis.

- Family practices can be associated with the impossibility of moving away, as restricted forms of mobility are brought about *because* of relationships. Family and intimate mobilities are not necessarily bound up with the ever-increasing speed of late modernity, but there are many circumstances where relationships bring about immobility. This is just as much about family mobility as studies of meetings and co-presence. Immobility can be voluntary, such as the acknowledgment of adult children and their now-dependent parent(s) of the need for proximity and co-presence, or en-forced, such as the victims of domestic abuse 'trapped' in a relationship.

- Mobility may be secret or illicit. Through mobilities we may hide aspects of our lives from others, have affairs or plot escapes and adventures. Intimacy is not always disclosed to others but can be hidden or even denied, and this may be channelled through mobility. The imaginary potential of mobility can further complicate the relationality of corporeal movement.

Thus the myriad different ways in which relationships are ordered and arranged across different geographical scales are of interest to sociologists and geographers, including LAT couples, commuter families, transnational families and so on. Mobility can create intimacy in new and diverse ways; in some of its forms, mobility decisions and practices are shaped by relationships, particularly for those who are marginalised by power structures and ideologies, for example the trailing spouse or child. In other forms, mobility facilitates breaking away from these same structures and helps to provide opportunities for more egalitarian intimate relations, which in turn are often sustained through intricate practices of hyper mobility (such as in dual-career families). Mobility practices therefore sustain relationships but also provide the opportunity for their demise and the formations of new intimacies. In addition, these mobile bodies, such as the trailing spouse, the commuter or LAT couples, though less figurative than the more well-worked subjects in the mobilities literature, such as the flâneur, the tramp or the tourist (see Merriman and Cresswell, 2008), can also move the mobilities turn on from this preoccupation with individual forms to focus not just on the mobile body or subject doing something but also on how these doings intersect with others. Focussing on idealised individual forms disguises the significance of the relationality of mobility. Yet one of the challenges of moving mobilities on from these singular subjects to more plural forms is that it is more straightforward to capture the figurative character of individual mobilities than collective forms because what is significant about the latter has less to do with the individual subjects and more to do with how mobilities interrelate.

In between the processes of formation and dissolution, mobility underscores the everyday practices of relationships; the time we spend together and the time we spend apart are framed through movement. This interplay between mobility and intimacy is also inherently dealing with the spatial and embodied quality of intimacy. Intimacy pertains to our interactions with significant others and is therefore dependent on our appropriation of and our use of space. Being intimate is spatially contingent because both co-presence and separation are fundamental to intimate relationships, as is the need for privacy, either alone or with an intimate partner – distance might make the heart grow fonder or it might drive couples apart. We need, therefore, to retain the active construction of intimacy, but not at the expense of losing sight of the importance of embeddedness and commitment.

Families on the move encapsulate a complex array of meanings, acknowledging the opportunities and the freedom as well as the restrictions of im(mobilities). However, I do not want to suggest that being on the move is either to be resisted or celebrated, as many forms of family mobility will combine elements of these different readings: thus commuting can be both mundane and expressive; holidays are times for adventures as well as arguments and boredom; and moving house is exciting and stressful, involving both farewells and new opportunities. At different times, one of these meanings might have more resonance than another: commuting becomes more of a drag and a commitment when combined with juggling childcare as well as work commitments; going on holiday with the family might provide a welcome period for parents to spend time with their children, which might be enjoyed by younger children but resisted by teenagers. Opening up family life to consider its mobile forms has the advantage of moving family beyond binary oppositions of decline versus stability, but rather points to the variability of family practices in both form and meaning.

The potential for widening the scope of mobilities through an engagement with family practices is quite considerable, but what about the opposite direction? That is, how can the mobilities turn invigorate family? At one level, mobilities can be seen as enriching practices but also intensifying them. Maintaining the dialectic between practice and structure that is retained in the practices approach can be difficult if we focus exclusively on the momentum of movement: that is, if mobility becomes ubiquitous in accounts of family life, family itself may be rendered insignificant. What a mobility approach can lend itself to is a recognition of the significance of origins and destinations and how these are brought together through mobility. Moreover, we need to be alert to mobility in terms of both time and space. One limitation of focussing on practice is that it can freeze family in time, and the importance of the everyday can emphasise the reproductive functionality of family practices rather than their emancipatory capacity. In other words, what I suggest here is that a missing piece of family practices is the mobility of the self through time as well as space, and that this corporeal mobility is a way of managing emotions. Time is more than a backdrop for family life; rather, as Elizabeth Grosz (1999: 4) expresses, time is an 'open-ended and fundamentally active force'. Our response to this force can be expressed by the need to move on and reconfigure family and intimate relations as well as the impossibility of bringing this about. Families do not stay still either in time or place: children grow up, leave home and move away, relationships end and family members pass away. These movements, while shaped by social, cultural and institutional practices, also create and reaffirm relationships and moral identities, for example the 'good' child who stays in touch or the 'neglectful' absent parent.

Family scholars are interested in these mobility events, and they are often conceptualised around the idea of transition from one form or state to another. This emphasis on transition can reify stasis, that is, the process of change is treated as temporary. For example academic interest in youth transitions can emphasise the end point of acquiring adult status rather than revealing the significance of the journey to this process, and this has generated considerable debate in youth studies (Wyn and Woodman, 2006). A mobilities perspective can challenge family scholars to consider the full potential of different forms of mobilities over different temporal and geographical scales that range from intra-domestic and other daily movements to longer-term migratory moves as well as those that are anticipated and imagined.

A final way in which mobilities could potentially invigorate family practices is through tying together spatial and social (im)mobility. A critique of family practices is that accounts of how family life is framed by social structures are lost through the focus on individual agency, even if this is not necessarily the intention of the practices approach. Yet mobilities are not experienced in isolation from each other and can bring about social change or reinforce social divisions; thus the outcome of family mobilities is not restricted to family members but is also bound up with wider social relations. Diana Leonard (1980), for example, discusses the practice of 'spoiling and keeping close' in a working-class community in Swansea, and keeping close can be linked to the assumed difficulties of both spatial and social mobility. Leonard's empirical findings contrast with Colin Bell's (1968) account of middle-class spiralists, who achieved social mobility through geographical mobility. A theme that will be returned to throughout this book is how tensions between individual and collective mobilities are structured by social identities, particularly class and gender.

Conclusion

A considerable amount has been written about the relationship between family and modernity, and debates about the possibilities and limitations of new intimacies and families of choice have continued in both academic and more populist arenas. At times this debate is circular and driven as much by an ideal of what family ought to be rather than what it is, with opposing sides lined up to champion conservative/traditionalist approaches versus more progressive and liberal forms. Part of this debate involves mapping the varied arrangements that might, or might not, be taken as representative of 'family' (see, for example, Stacey, 2011). Yet, at least in its structural form, the family in modern industrialised countries has not fragmented into multiple different types; in the United Kingdom the most common household type in 2010 was one family, consisting of a couple with or without children (ONS, 2011). Despite this, the limitations of focussing on structure are now well established in academic theory, and the need to envisage family through practices is widely accepted. Putting this vision into practice is, though, more challenging. My suggestion is that the synergy between family and mobility may provide a way of re-visioning the family that can move family beyond its structural form. Moreover, this theoretical approach does not always rely on mapping synergies and agreement; rather, a collision between the two can usefully shatter preconceptions in the way that Bernardes is attempting to do when he suggests that the family cannot exist. The fascinating thing about seeing family through mobility and vice versa is the extensive range of possibilities that this reveals. Family is no longer confined by either structure or locality (such as the domestic setting), and mobility can be broken out of a preoccupation with the doings of mobile subjects to consider the relationality of mobilities. Family mobilities are also multidirectional; that is, they can be either or both centrifugal and centripetal forces, involving both moving away and moving together. Family can therefore be placed in the centre of this multidirectional travel, but mobilities can also decentre family; the relationality of family mobilities is not restricted to a fixed network or structure, but flows between a complex and dynamic net of affinities. Moreover, some intimate mobilities can be illicit or unexpected and destabilise the centrality of family structure. This focus on relational mobilities also potentially provides a way of tying the meanings of mobility to points of departure and arrival. In the following chapters I map out the terrain of family and intimate mobilities, exploring how a re-visioning of family through mobilities can be used to interrogate established family practices, such as relationship formation, dissolution, leaving home, moving house, parenting and the negotiation of domestic spaces as well as to reveal aspects of family practices that have remained on the periphery of academic scholarship, such as holidays, courtship practices and children's mobilities.

3
Intimate Mobilities: Moving out, Moving in and Moving on

As I have outlined in the previous chapter, a key idea of the mobilities turn is not just to approach mobility as being the act of moving from A to B but also to consider how connections and relationships are created and sustained through mobility. The significance of mobility is apparent if we consider how, colloquially, the main stages and events of relationship formation are identified with movement such as 'going out', 'moving in' or 'moving on'. Mobility and intimacy are interdependent, as a change in one nearly always involves a change in the other. A working assumption about mobility and intimacy could be that the two are counter-opposed: we have to work to maintain intimacy despite mobility, as intimacy is dependent on corporeal co-presence that is diluted through mobility. Yet this assumption takes a rather fixed interpretation of mobility and intimacy; for example, mobility might force couples apart but it can also bring them back together. This suggests an alternative conceptualisation – that intimacy is formed, maintained and renewed by mobility and movement. Rather than treating mobility as an outcome of relationship flux, mobility can be seen to create opportunities for making new connections and relationships; put rather crudely, if we all stayed put then we would have very limited social circles and a restricted pool of potential partners. However, the opposite causality between mobility and relationships also holds: mobility can drive people apart and can be a causal factor in relationship breakdown.

In this chapter, I consider the interplay between intimacy and mobility, specifically the ways in which mobility both facilitates and brings about the processes of relationship formation and dissolution.

That a change in intimate relations almost always involves some form of mobility is not exactly a novel observation, and this is most readily conceptualised as the relationship between residential change and partnership formation. Yet this infers a rather static understanding of mobility, as it emphasises the point of change rather than the process of movement. Hence, while residential change is clearly important in framing intimate relations, there are other more subtle and less celebrated processes through which intimacy is formed and dissolved. While individual life courses are demarcated by events such as marriage, which are celebrated and recorded publicly as well as privately, these events are part of a longer chain of practices that might depend on, or produce, complex mobilities. Couples meet and form relationships, often in very unremarkable and mundane ways, that develop over time and space. In other words, the contribution of mobility to intimate relations is not just about residential change (buying a first house and moving in together) but relates to more subtle processes that are essential to how couples meet, sustain and maybe dissolve relationships. Hence, if our focus is on the *processes* of partnership formation rather than on the act of getting married or divorced, this suggests a different interplay with mobility that foregrounds the flux and flow of everyday life as opposed to more 'fixed' movements, such as residential change. Another way of conceptualising this approach is that it is about slowing down mobility and intimacy to their constituent practices and processes.

Thus, in this chapter, the conceptualisation of intimate mobility that I develop does not just relate to residential changes or migrations that come about as a result of or in anticipation of changes in intimate relations, but rather these one-off events are better understood as stages or mileposts in processes of sequences of more mundane or less celebrated events. It is also important to consider more hidden, forbidden or illicit mobilities that may bring about or unsettle intimate relations. So, rather than focussing on specific events, I use a life course framework to consider how mobility is interwoven into the processes and practices of intimacy (see Bailey, 2009). Another way of approaching the issue here is to say that it is about how individual mobility is bound up with the lives of others – young people leaving home experience changing relationships with parents as well as the opportunities to form new relationships with significant others; the formation of relationships and their dissolution is often brought about by individual mobilities. Thus, following Cresswell (2006) rather than adopting a more usual sedentary approach to intimacy that emphasises the friction between stability and separation, a nomadic reading of intimacy not just recognises the contribution of mobility to relationship formation but considers the interweaving of intimacy and movement over the life course.

The journeys of intimate relationships are often revealed in biographical form. Take, for example, the biographical account of Lorna, who was interviewed as part of a research project on motherhood and smoking in a disadvantaged community in Liverpool. When asked to talk about her life history, she framed it through mobility, acknowledging that most of her life had been spent 'like a gypsy', escaping from her parents, moving in with partners and moving associated with having children, until she returned to her 'home' neighbourhood:

> I was born in Walton, lived there until I was 10 with three sisters and my mom and dad. My mom was a cleaner and my dad worked in Ford's. We all went to school down Walton and loved it, loved school, loved Walton, loved the area, everything. We moved from Walton to Norris Green when I was 10 or 11. And we all grew up the same, you know, all the hand-me-downs, and all went to the same schools. One by one, my sisters, well the eldest two, got married, had babies, well, found out they were pregnant and got married, because my dad is a very strict, stern, stubborn man and if you have problems you have to get married straight away. So those two done that, and the next one didn't get pregnant, hasn't got married. I got pregnant at 18, which my dad wasn't too pleased about because I wasn't ready to get married at that young age. He chucked me out of the house. We moved; I moved, then. Oh, I moved to Huyton when I had had my eldest lad. Lived there for about four or five years and moved to Kensington and back to Huyton, and back to Kensington; I lived like a gypsy for many years and then finally got a house here, up by my parents, back where I want to be.

Lorna's narrative, and the way she presents it, emphasises the chaos of her mobility and the dialectical momentum between escape and return. Moreover, her intimate mobilities were not necessarily planned or chosen but came about through other events that, in turn, were interconnected. Thus when considering intimate mobilities it is important not to focus on a unidirectional process through the life course but to be alert to the varying momentum and direction of mobility. However, as an organising principle for developing a narrative of intimate mobilities, I structure my discussion of intimate mobilities over the life course to consider how it is impossible to conceive of the events of leaving home, courtship and marriage and its dissolution without considering movement and mobility.

Leaving home

Life course approaches often begin with a point of departure, and I start this account of intimate mobilities with the process of young people leaving the parental home. This account considers two dimensions: first, how has leaving home been assessed in a historical context, and second, what is its relevance to contemporary youth transitions? This review of historical and temporary processes reveals distinct ways in which leaving home has been conceptualised: historical accounts have treated leaving home as a process of family formation and fertility regulation, while contemporary accounts emphasise the relationship between leaving home and other transitions. Yet this distinction is not really that radical, in that the nexus of most scholar's accounts of leaving home is about discerning the balance between individual agency and structure, locating the act of individual departure within the context of social, economic and cultural contexts. Different historical timeframes highlight specific conditionalities, from the need to ensure household survival in medieval societies to the problems of high unemployment and rising housing costs facing young people in the twenty-first century. While my account acknowledges the significance of these debates, my interest is to consider the embodied practice of leaving home, how the very act of leaving (or not leaving) has implications for the self and other family members and what we can infer about the relationships between space, mobility, intimacy and identity from these practices.

Historical processes: Family, economy and mobility

Historical accounts of leaving home emphasise the spatial practices of marriage and partnership formation, as leaving home is usually treated as either an outcome or a precursor of marriage. Interestingly, despite the very public debates about the decline of marriage and its significance in late modernity, the focus on the institution of marriage is very much a modern idea. Thus if we want to consider marriage as a process rather than as an 'event', it is germane to consider how historians have written about marriage, as the idea of marriage as a process resonates in historical accounts of partnership and household formation. The dominant narrative of marriage in the historical literature identifies changes in the age of marriage as a key fulcrum by which fertility was regulated through the cultural practices of household formation (see, for example, Smith, 1981; Thornton, 2005; Laslett, 1965). The treatment of marriage as a key constituent in fertility regulation implicitly locates marriage within the processes of family formation, rather than an institution in its own right.

As well as the timing and universality of marriage, another important key debate in historical scholarship of the family relates to living arrangements. The contribution of key writers, from Le Play in the nineteenth century through to the empirical scholarship of Laslett and his colleagues at the Cambridge Group in the 1960s and 1970s and more recent comparative studies (see, for example, Goody, 1996; Ruggles, 2009), has been to debate the relationship between economic and cultural determinants of household formation. While this debate is conventionally interpreted as attempting to distinguish between distinctive living arrangements and how these vary over time and place, specifically the propensity to form intergenerational households, it can be turned around and rediscovered as a debate about mobility. While the historical tradition prioritises the distinctiveness of settlement patterns, their very existence depends on mobilities, and I suggest that it is possible to turn this account of family in past times inside out to reveal the mobilities of family formation as well as the structures. In the historiography of marriage and household formation, opportunities for youth mobility are key considerations in unpacking the patterns and practices of household formation (see, for example, Wall, 1978; Reher, 1998; Maddern, 2007). For example, to take Le Play's original typology of family types as being patriarchal, unstable and stem, these were distinguished by distinct mobility patterns, which in turn Le Play associated with distinctive intergenerational relations (Ruggles, 2010). Patriarchal families were the least dispersed, thus enabling the continuation of parental control; unstable families (which today would be classified as nuclear) were the most mobile, with couples establishing an independent residence at marriage and all adult children leaving this household to establish their own independent residences. Stem families, which Le Play particularly celebrated, were somewhat in between the two, with one child remaining in the parental home and the other children moving away (see Thornton, 2005). The importance of mobility and residential practices also underscored Hajnal's (1965) celebrated distinction between western- and eastern-European household formation (delimited by a line from Trieste to St Petersburg): older ages of marriage in the west were associated with young people leaving home and moving to a new locality prior to forming their own households. Once formed, these households were predominately nuclear, in contrast to the extended household form associated with younger and universal marriage in the east.

Differences in the timing and frequency of movements out of the parental home are considered as key data for delimiting the prevailing practices of household formation. The pattern of leaving home at young ages and delayed marriage is well documented in England (Schürer, 2004; Laslett, 1983; Pooley and Turnbull, 2004; Wall, 1987). Laslett's estimates of ages of individuals leaving home in early modern England suggest that young people left home between the ages of 12 and 20, though subsequent analysis suggests how this process was gradual. Though youth mobility was the 'norm', not all young people necessarily followed this pattern (Wall, 1987), and many early departures were followed by young people returning home (Pooley and Turnbull, 2004). Opportunities for employment were vital in supporting youth mobility, and in particular the institution of service supported the transfer of young people between households (Schürer, 2004). Throughout the latter half of the nineteenth century and the early decades of the twentieth, as opportunities for service contracted, leaving home practices shifted towards more homogeneous and contracted departures at older ages. Thus, while practices of leaving home in England have responded to changing economic and social conditions, it would seem reasonable to concur with Goldberg's observation, based on analysis of medieval records for York, that 'the young of both sexes were a singularly mobile group, indeed that mobility may be perceived as a facet of youth' (2004: 59). This depiction is apposite for different times and localities. It is not just the act of moving from A to B that mattered in relation to youth in medieval York; what is also significant is what could be achieved by young people through mobility.

The historical account of marriage and family formation identifies individual mobility as a key constituent practice, but also shows that this individual mobility is bound up with cultural practices of household formation as well as economic conditions. For young people, mobility was a way of starting out in life, and both economic and relational transitions depended on mobility. In later medieval Germany, for example, spending time as a journeyman (*Geselle*) involved moving from one locality to another to gain experience of different workshops and skills and was an essential part of training to become a master craftsman. The significance of youth mobility in past times is exemplified in Page Moch's (2003) authoritative review of migration from early modern to twentieth-century Europe, which is essentially a review of youth mobility. For Page Moch, mobility was a survival mechanism for families, as young people's migration sought not only to relieve the burden for peasant households of feeding all its adults members; in addition, the flow of remittances from those who moved away augmented household income. Thus she concludes that 'poverty, insecurity, and misfortune themselves sent people on the road. Stability was a privilege' (2003: 2).

Page Moch's account draws on detailed archival research, but also considers how popular folklore celebrated the importance and potential of youth mobility. There are many celebrations of mobility in popular folklore, but in England this tradition is best represented by the stories of Dick Whittington, who first appeared in stories dating from the early 1600s based on the life and times of a mayor in London in the late fourteenth and early fifteenth centuries, though history has certainly embellished his story. In folklore, Dick comes from a poor background to seek his fortune in London. Disillusioned, he leaves, only to be tempted back by hearing the bells of Bow church ringing out that he should return to become 'thrice Lord Mayor of London'. On his return, he does seek his fortune, though not in London, as his subsequent wealth is earned through a series of adventures trading overseas. Dick eventually marries a merchant's daughter and becomes mayor of London. Though the original Dick Whittington, on whom the story is based, did not come from a poor family but from a privileged merchant background, the idea that it is possible for someone born into poverty to hold one of the highest positions in the land is an enduring myth. Moreover, Dick achieved this through mobility: his rise to fame and fortune was secured through leaving home, returning to London and then leaving it again. Though in reality very few individuals could hope to emulate the legend of Dick Whittington, as Page Moch argues, most mobility was brought about by economic deprivation, and while mobility supported individuals and their families, it very rarely secured privilege or personal wealth. However, what is celebrated here is the potential for mobility to open up new opportunities for young people; thus, geographical and social mobility are intertwined. Yet this celebration of *individual* mobility was closely bound with families and households. As Macfarlane (1978) argues, for England the origins of individualisation were collective; practices of household formation depended on mobility practices; and the circular mobility of young people not only refreshed families and communities, but enabled some to achieve Whittington-style social mobility. Thus it is possible to use the analysis of both fictional and archival accounts of mobility that reveal the tension between the potential of moving away to enhance both personal and household resources and the fear of strangers within rural communities where encounters with outsiders were relatively infrequent.

This emphasis on the economic significance of mobility does not infer that historical accounts are narrated on the assumption of economic determinism. Rather, the emphasis is on the interplay between cultural and economic contexts. The tradition of historical family demography has focussed on identifying specific family systems in order to consider the interplay between cultural and economic practices. Thus, distinctive patterns of migration were predicated not just by economic conditions but on prevailing practices of household formation. For example, Reher's (1998) analysis of regional household formation patterns in Spain establishes how the Spanish family was characterised by complex regional diversity that cannot be reduced to stereotypical patterns, such as the distinction between stem or nuclear family households. This complexity had implications for the relationship between household formation and mobility. The mixing of different regional systems of inheritance, living arrangements and individual mobility led to uneven regional patterns of mobility. Thus mobility was not an automatic response to economic conditions:

who moved (for example, was it sons or daughters, older or young siblings?), where they moved to (that is, how far?) and for how long (seasonal or permanent mobility?) were negotiated with reference to cultural practices, household structure (that is, the demand for care within the home and the distribution of resources), prevailing economic conditions and access to land.

Contemporary practices of youth mobility

Mobility, not just as a way of escaping poverty, but as an essential precursor for marriage and household formation, is a consistent tableau in historical accounts of youth mobility. The historical record reveals the interplay between mobility, household and partnership formation, and employment for young people, though these connections have received less attention in relation to contemporary youth, and the significance of mobility is less prominent in contemporary accounts of youth transitions. This in part reflects an increasingly compartmentalised approach to youth that focuses on specific transitions, for example from school to employment, into and out of higher education and into parenthood and partnership, rather than seeking to explore the interplay between these transitions and how these are brought about by mobility (for reviews of youth transitions, see Jones, 2009; Furlong and Cartmel, 2007). Thus, in accounts of fragmented youth transitions, while the importance of place in framing young people's experiences is acknowledged, the significance of mobility is more muted. The conventional approach that has tended to shape transition research is one that emphasises how place of origin (and its intersection with class and other social identities) frames young people's experiences and ultimate destinations (see Roberts (2007) and Wyn and Woodman (2006) for discussion of the significance of the transition model in youth research). Thus interest in mobility and how young people use this as a resource (or constraint) in their personal lives and the significance of mobility for other transitions have received less attention. There are some noteworthy exceptions: Thompson and Taylor's (2005) analysis of longitudinal qualitative data concerning young people, collected over a five-year period, develops a distinction between cosmopolitanism and localism as a way of understanding young people's orientation to and experiences of mobility. Thompson and Taylor argue that it is futile to try to create typologies to understand young people's mobility (for example, to distinguish between movers and stayers), but rather that 'young people are torn between competing forces in relation to notions of home, tradition and fixedness on one hand and of mobility, escape and transformation on the other' (2005: 337). Thus, they foreground how mobility is imagined over its physical actuality; a cosmopolitan outlook is not restricted to those who travel, while other young people are very mobile yet retain their attachment to their home localities. Young people are differentiated in how they negotiate and acquiesce with these notions, and different young people in the same place will engage with mobility in distinctive ways. It is interesting to reflect that their distinctive methodology, which seeks to consider all aspects of young people's lives by following a group of young people over a long period, lends itself to analysis of mobility, which more conventional transitional approaches may conveniently ignore. Trying to make sense of youth mobility is a significant challenge for academic research, and one that does not lend itself to being able to classify young people into neatly demarcated groups and categories.

Scholarship on leaving home has sought to situate leaving home practices within their social, economic and cultural context (see, for example, Iacovou, 2002). However, within this framework there is a tendency to approach leaving home as a one-off event. This process is often regarded as an outcome of other transitions (for example, to university, for an employment or a partnership) rather than as a meaningful process in its own right that is bound up with changing relationships between young people and parents and provides opportunities for the formation of new intimacies and significant relationships. Yet, leaving home is often recognised by those involved, both parents and young people, as a symbolic process. Decisions about leaving home often incorporate a complex interplay of individual, generational and community mores that locate understandings of selfhood within a spatial domain.

In youth research, leaving home is conventionally taken as a marker of both moral and economic independence. Young people need a certain degree of financial resources (though in some situations, particularly for students leaving home, their parents are willing to support them) as well as the moral capacity to live by themselves. Of these two dimensions, the economic sphere has received most attention; that is, leaving home is often reduced to a question of resources, with the assumption that all things being equal both parents and young people would encourage spatial separation at an earlier age. Settersten and Ray's (2010) recent contribution does, though, provide a new perspective on this debate, as they suggest that a recent slowdown of youth transitions, epitomised by delayed departure out of the parental home in countries such as the United States, is a 'grown up' reaction to changing economic conditions in industrialised societies. Their contribution is just one of many self-help books targeted at parents and young people in the United States, some of which bemoan the apparent failure of American youth to have sufficient 'get up and go', while other contributions look for new opportunities in delayed transitions. At the very least this emerging interest in the timing of youth transitions reveals its significance and meaning beyond academic research, but also does little to dispel the idea that, fundamentally, what is really at issue here is the political economy of youth transitions. Furthermore, the expecta tion that vibrancy in youth is about action and mobility is one that is carefully controlled. Young people are exalted to live life to the full and to travel and experience as much as possible, and this is often contrasted with caricatures of youth that emphasise laziness and doing 'nothing'. However, when young people are mobilised in the form of protest or disorder, this very quickly brings about lockdown and the curtailment of youth mobilities. The surveillance of youth mobility by the police, and technologies such as mosquito devices that emit a high-pitched sound that is mostly only audible to young people to disperse them, contrasts with the popularisation of other forms of youth mobility and travel, such as gap years, backpacking and going away to university. There is at best an inconsistency in how certain forms of youth mobility are celebrated as epitomising the 'freedom' of youth, while other forms are regarded as dangerous transgressions.

The assumption that spatial independence is a prerequisite marker of the transition to adulthood is culturally specific, and this is illustrated in comparative research carried out by David Morgan and myself with young people and parents in Britain, Spain and Norway. While the differences between early-age- and later-age-leaving societies have been explored from a cultural and political perspective (see, for example, Iacovou, 2002; Aassve et al., 2002) and explanations of differences in the timing of leaving home have considered

the role of economic status, the state, family and other social structures (for example, the education system), the different ways in which
the leaving process is an articulation of how intimacy and the self
are developed in a spatial context has received less attention. In our
three case studies we found differences in how distance and closeness
were valued and prioritised in relationships between parents and children. Expectations about intimacy and distance are actively managed
through the process of leaving home. Many young people and parents negotiate a sense of the need to manage not being too close, but
at the same time not being too far away, and this balancing act was
reproduced in both young people's and parents' accounts. In some
contexts, closeness was prioritised in order to facilitate not just emotional support within families but also practical support. Moving
out but remaining in the same complex, street or neighbourhood
was a desired and often realised practice in a Spanish context. Living close to parents sustained day-to-day interactions, such as eating
meals together, shopping for each other and generally spending time
together.

Norwegian families, not surprisingly, provide a striking contrast
to the Spanish case studies in which the management of distance
and leaving home was a considered process and one in which parents recognised they had a role to play. Many Norwegian parents
expressed strong commitment to supporting children, not spoiling them, memorably expressed by two parents who said that they
'should not sew a pillow under their children's arms', that is, parents should not be too protective of their children and try to cushion
all of their falls. Spatial separation is an essential part of this process, but it begins in the home, before leaving. Young people were
encouraged to take responsibility for themselves and to engage in
household chores, and thus to have some experience of managing responsibility prior to leaving. Many parents and young people,
though, recognised that leaving home required a certain degree of
distance between two residences. One Norwegian mother described
how, ideally, her daughter should live at a distance meant that she
'would need to wear a coat' to visit her daughter's house – that is,
close enough for the mother to walk to, but far enough away for
them not to be living in each other's pockets. The use of metaphors is
quite striking in many of the Norwegian accounts and hints at how
shared understanding of separation is encouraged and maintained,

and that there are moral sanctions that govern an 'ideal' leaving home experience.

Leaving home transitions are therefore closely linked to our expectations of how intimacy and distance are spatially contingent, but this interplay is culturally contingent. Being physically 'too close' in some contexts is regarded with suspicion as indicative of being emotionally too much involved in either parents' or children's lives. In contrast, for many Spanish parents and young people, both men and women alike, physical closeness was an important characteristic of family support and interdependency. I shall return to consider the spatial practices of intimacy for different kinds of relationships in Chapter 6, as clearly the interactions between intimacy, mobility and co-presence are not just restricted to the relationship between older children and parents, but permeate all forms of intimacy.

We should, though, be cautious in assuming that leaving home necessarily means achieving independence, as closer inspection reveals that this is not necessarily the case. Consider, for example, leaving home to live with a partner or to get married; for women this movement could mean swapping one form of dependency for another. Adele, who we interviewed in Liverpool, described how, in leaving her parental home to live with her boyfriend (Gary), she had given up the freedom and 'independence' that she had enjoyed while living at home:

> but sometimes I feel that I had more independence being at home from what I do even living with Gary. I don't know. Whereas, when I was living at home I just used to see Gary on certain nights, and those other nights were mine – free to do whatever I wanted: go out to my mates, go and see my family, go and do whatever.

Adele goes on to describe how the expectation that she has to take responsibility for the housework in her new home has generated a feeling of resentment and of being trapped by the situation. Yet not everyone equates looking after others and responsibility with a lack of independence. Emma, also from Liverpool, described her reluctance to leave home as she felt very close to her mother and was aware of how much she helped her out by looking after her younger brothers and sisters as well as helping financially from time to time. Her mother, however, while recognising how much Emma contributed at home and that she was dependent on Emma in many ways, expressed her uneasiness about the situation. In particular, she talked about how guilty she felt about the situation and that by not leaving home Emma did not have the opportunity to become 'independent' and enjoy a period of youthful freedom:

> I think I lean on her too much; I really feel sometimes I'm doing what my mum did to me, and that's in many ways why I would have liked her to have gone away because she'd have had the space to do her own thing and have her own time.

Moreover, this pattern of matriarchal intergenerational support repeats down the generations, as Emma's mum supported her mother in the same way that Emma does now.

The stereotypical interpretation of leaving home as a one-way process from dependence to independence masks the complexity of how generational relations are sustained. In particular, it ignores the potential for intergenerationality – that the relationship between parents and children is not one-way; it is not just about young people establishing their own identity, facilitated by spatial distance. Rather, both parents and young people contribute to the process, and responsibility may be based on sharing space and supporting others rather than on distance and separation.

In conclusion, both popular ideals and academic research have foregrounded the importance of corporeal mobility in youth transitions, that is, that the very act of leaving home and moving away is a vital stage in the transition to adulthood. Moving away is popularly regarded as a precursor for both emotional maturity and economic advancement. Young people might not be told that the streets of London are paved with gold anymore, but they are expected to demonstrate their capabilities through mobility. Yet as I have argued in relation to the experiences of English students in higher education (Holdsworth, 2006, 2009), our faith in mobility and the ways in which movement is emblematic of achieving adulthood is, in some cases, misplaced. Going away to university is often a relatively smooth and ordered process where many of the decisions, such as finding somewhere to live, are taken care of, particularly for students moving away to live in residential halls. Students are not necessarily achieving economic independence, and in the era of 'helicopter parents', who manage their children's lives from a distance, not all young people who move away can claim emotional independence. In contrast, some students who stay at home do so because of caring needs at home or because of obligations within their home localities. Moreover, home-based students often have to negotiate complex daily commutes and move between very different communities, particularly between university and home neighbourhoods where going on to higher education is not necessarily valued (Christie, 2007; Holdsworth, 2009). Being local may signify a lack of imagination or the capabilities to move away, but it can also be a choice of young people who are negotiating complex family and/or community ties. Echoing Thompson and Taylor (2005), young people's orientation to mobilities is not necessarily correlated with their actual mobility. Local students can have a cosmopolitan outlook and can achieve the economic and emotional independence that their mobile peers are assumed to acquire through the very act of their mobility. The assumption that youth is about anticipating or realising mobility holds for different cultural and historical contexts. Though realised mobilities are varied and structured by social identities, the idea that the transition between child and adult is demarcated by mobility is unvarying. Yet this should not infer that this liminal period of mobility ends in stasis, but rather that it is a time of heightened mobility that foregrounds the interplay between mobility, intimacy and space. Mobility is heightened at times of transition. However, this does not mean that mobility is aligned linearly; the significance of developing a life course approach is that it is *not* presumed to depend on a uni-directional pathway. Studies of young people's mobility illustrate this circular movement and that young people do develop networks with others that are dispersed (Larsen et al., 2006). The patterns of individual mobility leave a trace, or a 'relational' imprint on the localities visited, and develop links with new places as, in turn, others move to new places or return home.

Courtship and marriage

A socio-cultural understanding of leaving home can reveal the symbolic significance of youth mobility in shaping young people's relationships with parents, but this mobility is also associated with young people forming new intimacies. While the historical account of leaving home tends to position departure from the family home as an initial first stage in this process, for contemporary youth the interplay between mobility and intimacy is more complex. Some young people may leave home in order to live with a partner, while for others departure from the parental home occurs before young people enter into new relationships. However, other than rather crude national comparisons of leaving home transitions that compare the proportion of young people who move out to get married/live with a partner to those who live in non-family/partnership living arrangements, the significance of mobility for partnership formation has received very little attention.

While the act of getting married and moving in together is an important staging point and one that is celebrated in all cultures, the events leading up to this event are usually less remarkable. We might describe this as practices of courtship, though this descriptor is itself rather historical and suggests a rather old-fashioned view of relationship formation, or it might bring to mind a more biological interpretation associated with the elaborate routines of mating animals. Yet while in contemporary modern societies a specific stage of 'courting' might seem old-fashioned, it still remains the case that couples have to meet and get to know each other before forming a relationship, something that nowadays is most commonly referred to as 'seeing someone'. Moreover, these practices of 'courtship' are essentially mobile. From providing opportunities for couples to meet for the first time as well as developing and sustaining intimate relationships, falling in love is often contingent on mobility and on the appropriation of space.

As with leaving home, in order to develop a sense of the significance of spatial practices in courtship the historical record is more rewarding. For example, Claire Langhamer's (2007) analysis of courtship in mid-twentieth-century England, drawing mainly on Mass Observation data, reveals how the everyday practices of courtship provided a rite of passage for young people, particularly in the context of near-universal nuptiality. Courtship presented young people with 'bounded opportunities' not just to meet suitable partners, but through these practices to 'perform and refine new gender roles, whilst simultaneously permitting the renegotiation of social status and identity' (2007: 176). Langhamer's account of courtship practices explores how young people were able to take advantage of new opportunities, particularly during the Second World War, and how women in particular were redefining their role in relationship formation. She draws attention to the significance of the geographical mobility of young people during the war and how it served 'to remove young people from the control of family and neighbourhood and allowed them access to a far greater range of potential partners' (ibid: 186). What is distinctive about this period, according to Langhamer, is the loosening of parental control over young people; as a consequence, young people were less likely to meet partners through family and social circles than through going to parties or in public spaces, such as cinema and pubs, that were celebrated as places for young people to meet.

The freedom that young people could exercise in their mobility and relationships contrasts with how this was regulated in earlier times, particularly for the middle and upper classes. We are familiar with the courtship rituals of Georgian and Victorian aristocracy through how these are represented in literature, particularly how the tensions between desire and constraint were managed. Managing mobilities, particularly women's mobility, is key here. Take, for example, the practice of employing chaperones for young women to avoid the possibility of indiscretion or the staging of the London Season around the display of debutantes at 'coming out' balls; through these, the intimate mobilities of women were regulated and controlled. For couples wishing to escape this control, the option was to elope, or runaway to get married. For couples in England, the legal regulation of marriage required publication of intention to marry (the publishing of banns); if couples did not have parental approval, this could be circumvented by eloping to Scotland, where notification was not required. Similar practices developed in the United States, where requirements for blood tests prior to marriage and notification of intention to marry varied between different states. While the legal cause for elopement may have diminished, the romantic ideal of running away to get married has not, though the moral status of a 'quickie' marriage remains ambivalent.

To return to Britain in the 1940s and 1950s, one aspect of courtship that emerged during this time was the tension of being intimate in public spaces and how this was resolved through leisure activities that were integral to courtship practices. Young people would appropriate urban space to 'parade' in and make introductions. For example, in

Manchester the practice of 'monkey-walking' was carried out in designated spaces on a Sunday evening to provide an opportunity for 'sexual display and performance' (ibid: 183). Going walking and/or to dances also provided opportunities for couples to meet and spend time together. Courtship often involved physical activity as a way of developing intimacy in the confines of public space. The slang and jargon that couples used to describe these activities hinted at their mobility. Couples referred to ' "stepping out", "walking out", and "going out": all terms which reflected the extent to which intimacy was developed in public and increasingly performed within the parameters of developing leisure opportunities' (ibid: 181).

Langhamer's account reveals the tension between public and private courtship practices and how appropriation of space through these mobile practices of courtship enabled young people to develop private intimacy within the 'public' practices of courtship. However, the time period from the 1930s to the 1950s is distinctive, in that it can be regarded as a 'golden era' for courtship, when young people had more freedom and choice and were able to meet members of the opposite sex away from direct parental control; yet at the same time the formation of relationships remained a carefully scrutinised 'public' process.

After the war the formation of heterosexual relationships was associated with increased sexual freedom for men, but particularly for women, who were able to assert more agency within relationships. The extensive literature on intimacy in late modernity identifies the capacity for new forms of reflective intimacy but also the limitations to individual agency and practice – heterosexual relationships in particular are bounded by carefully negotiated practices and identities. Yet the contribution of changing mobility and spatial practices to intimacy has not featured prominently in understanding changing forms of intimacy. Meah et al.'s (2008) cross-generational study of the making of heterosexual relationships, based on in-depth case studies of families in East Yorkshire, identifies that men's access to cars and motorbikes in the 1970s changed young people's scope for sexual intimacy compared to older generations. Though they do not expand on how the contribution of car ownership has changed sexual practices, the use of the car in sexual practice has a long history. The eroticism of the car is frequently promoted in advertising, while its use in voyeuristic sexual practices is not uncommon (Bell, 2006).

Young people in particular have used the car as a space to 'make out' free from parental surveillance (Sheller and Urry, 2000). As Bell concludes, what is significant here is how the use of the car challenges the dichotomy between public/private space and how that distinction is 'folded' by these practices (see also Hubbard, 2001). While both Hubbard and Bell focus on more '"scary" heterosexualities' (Hubbard, 2001: 57) that are not necessarily part of more mainstream sexual practices, the more mundane contribution of the car to young people's sexual initiation and partnership formation has received less attention.

It would seem reasonable to conclude that while the spatial practices of youth in the inter-war period focussed on the appropriation of public space, increased private mobility in the latter half of the twentieth century allowed for more opportunities for private intimacy and the practice of sex in 'folded' spaces that transcended the public–private divide. Heteronormativity is not just, though, dependent on the practice of sex, but is one that is (re)produced over generations as young people seek to escape adult control in their re-negotiated heterosexual identities. However, young people, when they have their own children, will use these experiences to develop their own strategies to regulate their children's sexual encounters and identities. Mobility and distance are implicit in how these identities are negotiated, and young people's claims to adult status are distinguished by 'possessing knowledge about sex, engaging in new embodied practices, experiencing bodily changes, and creating physical distance between oneself and the parental home' (Meah et al., 2008: 472).

Clearly, scale is an unacknowledged consideration here. Some young people might not have to travel very far to escape parental control, while others might want to put more distance between themselves and their parents. Sometimes this might reconcile with young people identifying distances that are far enough, but not too far from parents. For example, in relation to English students going to university, the 'right distance' is popularly referred to as the 'doughnut' effect, as students look for places to move to within a certain distance from the parental home – not too far away, but not too close. In terms of how far one has to move to meet new partners, this cannot be quantified. We can observe very different extremes, from 'catalogue brides' in Russia and East Asia who travel to Britain to marry, to moving to the next town. What matters here is not distance, but unfamiliarity and moving beyond one's immediate social circle.

This discussion of scale and distance might take on a different meaning for other intimate relationships. For example, the significance of strategies for negotiating parental control for heterosexual relationships may need revision for lesbian, gay, bisexual and transgender (LGBT) relationships. The transition out of the parental home can be particularly poignant for young people if it allows for an expression of their sexuality that is denied at home. Yet for many young people this point of departure is by no means smooth, and it often involves considerable risk and uncertainty. High incidences of homelessness among LGBT young people have been identified in both North America and the United Kingdom, and they reveal the problems facing these young people and the need for a policy response (Cull et al., 2006; O'Connor and Molloy, 2001). In qualitative research with young, homeless LGBT people, many associate their sudden departure from the family home either because their parents could not come to terms with their sexuality or because they feared that their parents would act in this way and sought to avoid this conflict by leaving home. While the overall prevalence of LGBT homelessness is very difficult to assess in some metropolitan districts of the United States, an estimated 25 per cent of all homeless young people are LGBT, whereas in the United Kingdom, studies around one-third of LGBT young people report housing problems (Cull et al., 2006: 16–17). Thus the ideal that mobility accommodates a progressive development of intimacy, in which young people can 'experiment' in the folded spaces between public and private that are accessed through mobility, is a heteronormative ideal. For many LGBT young people, mobility is far more abrupt, and coming out may require a physical relocation. I do not intend to create a dichotomy between LGBT and heterosexual intimacy, as clearly individual experiences will vary widely. It would, though, appear reasonable to assume that mobility practices of relationship formation and sexual intimacy are shaped by prevailing sexual norms.

So far I have focussed on Western practices of marriage and courtship, which privileges both privacy and individual choice. In other cultural and economic contexts the mobility practices of marriage and courtship may be quite different. For example, the difficulties facing couples – wanting to spend time together and be intimate – in the overcrowded cities in the global south are often overlooked in more advantaged contexts. But in cities such as Mumbai, this is a very real challenge and one that is further complicated by strict cultural norms governing the display of intimacy in public. The spaces that couples seek out in Mumbai include public parks (especially in the rainy season where umbrellas can be useful for privacy), cinemas, restaurants and taxis (Satalkar, 2012; see also Butcher, 2011). The mobilities associated with relationship formation are also distinctive. The practice of elopement, which, as I have discussed above, often romanticised in Western contexts as the triumph of love over parental control, is for many women in the Indian subcontinent their only option to escape violence at home. Women who run away to marry are not just resisting traditional societal structures, but their challenge to parental authority cuts them off from the main source of emotional and financial support (Raval et al., 2010). Other young people may enter into arranged marriages, and as such their mobility maybe forced rather than chosen. In this context, individual mobility is required to bring about allegiances between families as much as developing intimacies.

Mobilities associated with courtship practices and 'seeing' other people are, in most cases, very fluid rather than purposeful; in some situations they are extreme, such as running away to be with another person or to escape parental or community sanctions; and in other contexts they are more serendipitous. Mobility can also be an aim for the outcome of relationship formation, in terms of both its geographical and social forms, and this may be sought by the couple and/or other family members.

Partnership dissolution

Mobility is not only implicated in providing opportunities for young people's intimacies; another important observation of Langhamer's account of the courtship during the Second World War is how geographical mobility not only facilitated young people's relationship formation due to their ability to 'escape' parental control, but that this mobility also increased the opportunity to meet new partners. This understanding of mobility appeals to an appreciation of how movement opens up new opportunities and new connections. Yet there is also an intriguing paradox here in that movement is also associated with undermining an individual's ability to 'make commitments'. Thus while Langhamer associates geographical mixing with more opportunities *for* relationships, in societies with greater population 'churn', relationship dissolution is more common. This argument has received some support from ecological studies of the relationship between population turnover and divorce, particularly in the United States where there is a correlation between 'frontier' communities in the west and higher rates of relationship breakdown (Boyle et al., 2008). Too much freedom and mobility might therefore undermine intimacy and commitment, or it could be that more mobile individuals are more likely to experience relationship breakdown, though the actual causality of this correlation cannot easily be established. The interplay between mobility and relationship formation is therefore both dynamic and contradictory. Moreover, these interactions do not just play out in communities but are interwoven into individual life course trajectories. In most contemporary societies, increasing rates of partnership breakdown and divorce are associated with re-partnership and remarriage. While couples today might find it harder to sustain relationships over a lifetime, the high rate of remarriage and re-partnership confirms how individuals are still committed to the ideal of love and intimacy.

As I outlined in Chapter 2, the apparent fragility of contemporary relationships has received considerable attention from political as well as academic commentators. Putting to one side the moral and social implications of relationship flux, what is of interest for my purpose here is how mobility is implied, not just in the formation of relationships, but in how they are sustained and also dissolved. Yet the observation that mobility is implicated in both the formation and dissolution of relationships is not just relevant to contemporary modern societies. Maddern (2007) argues that in medieval England geographical mobility facilitated a cycle of marriage formation and 'dissolution' that allowed couples to circumvent ecclesiastical court procedures, and that rather than being stable and monogamous, for many poor people marriage was experienced as serial bigamy:

> In circumstances of such high geographical mobility, especially for those forced to move to seek work, long-term marital relationships may have been hard to sustain, while conditions were clearly favourable for those wishing to move from one

marital relationship to another without coming under the intense scrutiny either of censorious and long-term neighbours, or of intrusive ecclesiastical regulation.

(Maddern, 2007: 91)

Thus the practices of mobility that stimulated household formation for young couples were carried onwards, and for some facilitated subsequent partnership and household dissolution. The necessity of taking a longer view of the interplay between mobility and relationships over the life course, rather than focussing on how mobility brings about discrete events, would appear to be relevant in pre-modern contexts. Maddern's observation of the fragility of medieval marriages can be carried forward into late modern societies, and it is possible to quantify the relationship between mobility and relationship breakdown. Flowerdew and Al-Hamad's (2004) analysis of the Household Sample of Anonymised Records for Great Britain reveals that divorced adults are more migratory than others, but that these moves are more likely to be over short distances. Thus the end of relationships is associated with a high frequency of short-distance residential changes, which in turn are often linked with the formation of new relationships.

Yet individual mobility is not just a consequence of partnership formation and dissolution, or indicative of relationship flux. There is another dimension to divorce and mobility – that mobility may be a causal factor for relationship breakdown. In other words, we should consider if more mobile individuals, and this might include those involved in different forms of mobility, from residential change to long-distance commuting, may find it harder to sustain relationships over the distances implied by their mobility. It is probably easier to conceptualise this relationship with reference to residential change; after all, moving house is popularly regarded as one of the most stressful events in contemporary life, so does the stress of moving influence the quality of relationships? Evidence of the detrimental impact of mobility on intimate relations is provided by analysis of longitudinal data on the impact of mobility on divorce. This research area starts out with the premise that moving is a stressful time. The actual process of moving is recognised as causing anxiety and strain for all those involved, and if this involves more than one person, then clearly the potential for an impact on relationships should not be discounted. Hence, while individual mobility may be beneficial for individuals, the impact on family and other intimate relations is more contestable (I discuss the tensions inherent in family mobility in Chapter 4). To date, research has considered the impact of transnational migration on divorce. Boyle et al.'s (2008) analysis of Austrian longitudinal data also confirms that migration is a risk factor for relationship breakdown (the choice of Austria for analysis of the relationship between partnership dissolution and mobility was influenced by the availability of appropriate data, which remains one of the main hurdles for demographic analysis of mobility and family processes). There are two significant findings from this analysis. First, that the first long-distance moves are not associated with an increase risk of partnership dissolution; rather, it is frequent moves (two or more), especially over long distances, that put strains on relationships. The second observation is that moving from an urban area to a rural one is not associated with the same increased risk. There are clearly policy implications here, for example companies involved in relocating staff could take into account the significance of mobility on their employees' well-being and relationships.

It could be assumed from the analysis of migration and divorce that the impact on relationships is an unintended outcome of mobility, and in seeking to make sense of this finding we might consider the impact of the 'stresses' of mobility, for example buying a house, moving school and so on. However, other accounts of the impact of mobility on relationships also acknowledge the complexity of mobility and intimacy. Ideals about escaping to make a better life (usually from an urban to a rural community) receive considerable coverage in contemporary media. For example, UK television has a number of reality programmes that follow couples seeking to make a new life somewhere 'better'. These accounts, though, are often keen to point out how ambitious mobility plans can challenge 'stable' relationships. Reality TV programmes do not meet the requirements of rigorous empirical analysis, as the point of these programmes is entertainment, where we can vicariously experience another more mobile life from a sedentary viewer's armchair. But we can at least acknowledge that mobility has the potential to both undermine and sustain relationships, and that the outcome of mobility for relationships is not always intended. Mobility may be serendipitous or destabilising for intimate relationships.

Moving on, unplanned departures and illicit mobilities

I began this account of intimate mobilities by reflecting on the historical account of household formation, and what it reveals about the significance of mobility patterns. One limitation of this approach is that it emphasises the strategic potential of mobility: individual mobility ensures the survival of existing households as well as the formation of new ones. Yet mobility can also be an escape: running away from home, eloping or walking out on a relationship are not always negotiated or considered departures. These kinds of experiences are often romanticised and are associated with breaking free from family or relationship ties and starting again somewhere else or with someone new. There is no shortage of examples from popular culture that resonate with this ideal. Take, for example, the character Ryan Bingham played by George Clooney in the film *Up in the Air*. Ryan leads the ultimate mobile life travelling around the United States for his job (which is to sack employees), living out of a suitcase and without commitments. However, Ryan's unplanned mobility goes against this ideal of having no ties and being constantly mobile when he decides on a whim to attend his sister's wedding with a woman he has started a 'mobile' relationship with. This mobility sets in train a series of events and journeys which challenge Ryan's belief in a life with no commitments. Thus, Ryan's unplanned mobility is about acknowledging the importance of belonging and relationships, though in the end he remains single and nomadic.

While *Up in the Air* does not provide the 'happy ending' of romantic love and stability, the lead character remains in control of his mobility. But not all running away is about chasing dreams or meeting people, and the reality is often very different, especially for young people. In the United Kingdom, the National Society for the Prevention of Cruelty to Children [NSPCC] reports that around 77,000 children aged under 16 run away from home every year, and that among these runaways, on average, one in eight young people are physically hurt and one in nine sexually assaulted while they are away. Young people who run away are likely to be running away from care or an abusive family home. To run away is often, therefore, an extreme choice in response to circumstances from which strategic departures are not possible. Yet while there are clearly identifiable risk factors for young people running away, especially those running away from care, who are more likely to be repeat escapees, it is not these risk factors that bring these children to the attention of local services, but their realised mobility. As Malloch and Burgess (2011: 72) point out, 'young runaways are often viewed as "vulnerable" or "at risk" by the act of running away rather than as a result of the factors which prompted them to run'. It is the act of escape that signifies vulnerability, rather than the choice of staying put and suffering these risks.

It is important not just to dwell on the emancipatory potential of intimate mobilities, as these can be threatening and controlling. Mobility can be used as a way of intimidating others, as the harrowing experiences of female victims of stalking illustrates. In the United Kingdom, the Home Office estimates that there are 120,000 cases of stalking every year (Russell, 2012) and that the majority of victims are women. The act of stalking, with its resulting fear of being followed and the intimidation this causes, is a way of asserting power through mobility, rather than through restricting individual movement, though the end result for many women makes them fearful of their own mobility.

Intimate mobilities are not always the preoccupation of those at the beginning of the life course, but they are interwoven throughout individual and collective trajectories. Though mobilities undertaken at older ages are less celebrated than ones associated with youth, this should not mean they are less significant. Moving as a later-life couple, often post-retirement, is often associated with a desire to start afresh once the demands of negotiating work and family are dissipated. Mobility throughout the life course can therefore be seen as important in reinvigorating relationships. Moreover, the opportunity to move after retirement is often a wished-for and planned activity. Yet moving on cannot always be planned if it is predicated by events out of one's own control. For example, the death of a partner and subsequent loss is associated with mobility. Again, the significance of movement is revealed in colloquialisms: we talk about the need to 'move on'; though this does not always involve a physical mobility, the ideal is often that both physical movement and an emotional journey go hand in hand. Analysis of the dynamics of housing over the life course demonstrates that widowhood is associated with a greater propensity to move, particularly at older ages (Bonnet et al., 2010). At older ages, mobility is associated with the need to downsize but also with a move closer to other family members, particularly children; thus childless widow(er)s are less likely to move than those with children. Once again, the mobility of individuals is closely bound with relationships with others, in this case intergenerational relationships. The figure of the pensioner abandoned at home with no one to care for and whom no one visits is often referred to in discourses of community decline. Yet scholarship on communities and networks at older ages reveals how emotional attachment both to home and to the surrounding community can be magnified by age, and that communities of older people are resilient (Phillipson et al., 2000). It is too simplistic to assume that community at older ages is associated with immobility and of having lived in place for a long time; rather, the times when children leave home or retirement are often the kinds of interruptions that bring about mobility and invigoration of social affinities.

Not all intimate mobilities are visible, as intimacies are also formed and maintained through more hidden practices. The complexity of intimate relationships includes unrequited love, love triangles, extramarital affairs and virtual relationships, all of which are dependent on mobility in some form or another, be it imaginative or corporeal. Moreover, the invisibility of these mobilities may be part of the attraction of the relationship. Having a secret life, which can now be virtual as well as real, may also be one way of sustaining more visible forms; that is, it provides a way of escaping more public intimacies. There is considerable interest in the potential of virtual second lives and ways in which people form relationships, and dissolve them, online (see, for example, Turkle, 2011). Yet secrecy and distance can also be threatening: while virtual relationships might be regarded as 'safe', the need to protect one's identity online reflects the fear that if these relationships are materialised then this might put one in considerable danger.

Conclusion

I began this chapter with the observation that changes in intimate relationships will almost always involve some form of mobility, and the inevitability of this change has only recently been explored by social scientists. While the significance of mobility for intimacy is hinted at in popular colloquiums used to describe the process of courtship, relationship formation and dissolution, this significance has received less academic attention. Researching mobility associated with life course events has remained a sub-discipline of population geography. Yet this narrow perspective on life course mobility is now being challenged. First, it is too simplistic to treat mobility as an outcome of life course events: mobility clearly also facilitates and changes these events, and moreover the desire to move is often a reason for changing relationships; wanting to move 'on' involves consideration of both attachment to intimate relations and locality. Moreover, while mobility associated with key events is not necessarily strategic, mobility decisions cannot be reduced to rational decision making. There is a tension between the desire and opportunity to either stay put or leave. Yet we also need to be wary of overplaying this tension, as mobility in the form of moving on and forming new relationships is a precursor to settling down, as Laura described in her discussion of her 'gypsy' life and eventual return home. But precisely because mobility is so much a part of relationship formation and dissolution, it is possible to overlook its contribution, or at least just treat mobility as a product of relationship change. In other words, mobility is so ubiquitous that we not only fail to acknowledge it, but extracting movement out of intimacy can be rather artificial and clumsy. I suggest that instead we need to consider intimacy through mobility and vice versa, and that this should not just focus on the moment of mobility, but on how this mobility is brought about and its implications.

As we start to think through this idea of mobility *through* intimacy and vice versa, this challenges us to recognise the complexity of mobilities and our understanding of partnership and other intimate relationships. Using a mobility lens to understand relationships accentuates relationships as a process, rather than referring to fixed states. It also unsettles the preoccupation with transition in the life course, as this conceptualisation focuses attention on the point of change rather than the process, and this limitation of the transition approach has been well debated in youth studies and increasingly in gerontology. Yet it is not just at the younger and older ends of the life course that the dynamics of intimate mobilities are relevant. Though youth in particular is associated with a heightened sense of mobility associated with leaving home, forming relationships and 'settling down', it is not a precursor to a period of immobility. Intimacies dissolve and change over time and space in both visible and invisible ways. Thus, the processional quality of the life course should not overshadow other conceptualisations of mobility that do not assume a linear or rational direction. Mobility is a way of moving on, often abruptly, and can bring about unexpected change, but it can also mean return. Mobility speeds up and slows down intimacy, but the reverse is also true: desires to go and stay are almost always framed by the formation, continuation and dissolution of intimate relationships.

The movement of individuals is intrinsic to both the maintenance of and reconfiguration of relationships. Yet to describe these as individualised mobilities is partial, as ultimately these are bound by collective experiences and settings. This shift between collective and individual is not clearly demarcated, because at certain times, such as leaving home, individual practices may dominate. The next two chapters follow this theme in foregrounding the collective quality of family and intimate mobilities, which may refer to mobilities carried out as a group or mobilities to sustain collective affinities.

4
Families on the Move I: Moving House and Commuting

If family is a verb, rather than a noun, it would seem reasonable to assume that family practices generate mobility and movement on different spatial and temporal scales. These practices can be viewed, as outlined in Chapter 3, from an individual perspective across the life course, yet we also need to take into consideration the intersections of individual mobilities with other doings and structures. My suggestion here is that while the mobilities turn has been about mobilising previously understood fixed and immobile bodies, communities, institutions and publics, the focus has very much been around the mobile body/subject *doing*; thus, a decentring away from the mobile body to its intersection with others is a much-needed development of the mobilities turn. In this and the subsequent chapter, I turn to consider intimate and family mobilities from a collective orientation. There are inevitable overlaps with the previous chapter in terms of key events, such as partnership formation, childbirth and dissolution, but the intention here is to consider the relationality of mobility practices. I consider the mobility of individual family members, which sustains family life, as well as occasions where families move together. The moves can be uni-directional, circular, permanent or transitory. I also consider how the interplay between family practices and mobility itself is subject to change, as families are reconfigured in response to life course events – such as childbirth, children leaving home and partnership dissolution – and changes in family members' personal circumstances such as job change or loss. However, making sense of the complexity of these interrelations is far from straightforward. One of the key issues is how the tension between individual choices and family practices is often resolved in relation to or is dependent on mobility. Mobility can challenge family life (for example, decisions to relocate may have different impacts on individual family members), sustain family life (the challenges of meeting individual needs can be sustained through complex mobility practices) or, in contrast, family practices may reduce opportunities for individual mobility (that is, meeting collective family needs may reduce individual opportunities for mobility). Clearly here, we are thinking about different temporal and spatial scales of mobility, from long-distance permanent residential change to daily commuting patterns. Moreover, mobility is not just implicated *by* family change and flux, but movement itself creates opportunities for both reaffirming and resolving family relationships.

The focus of this chapter and Chapter 5 is to unpack more collective forms of family mobility. This chapter focuses on more mainstream academic concerns with residential change and intra-familial mobility, primarily around commuting. The intention is to explore the interrelationship between economic and family life and how this reveals the structure and gendering of family life. This discussion opens up the possibility that family immobility is often sustained by individual mobility. A key theme throughout is the connection between mobility and migration or more temporary and fixed forms of movement. While scholarship has tended to focus on one of these dimensions, an overarching theme to be developed is how temporary and permanent movements over different geographical scales are interlinked.

Family migration and residential change

In making sense of the complexity of family mobility, I start with those more conventional understandings of family mobility – that is, migration and residential change. For demographers and population geographers, research on the spatial dynamics of family formation and intimate relations has been thwarted for two interconnected reasons. First, until recently demographic analyses of family formation has been more focused on family and household structure rather than on processes, and second, the lack of available longitudinal data on mobility and family processes has limited the kinds of demographic analysis that can be done. Yet these barriers to a more integrated approach to life course and mobility are increasingly being challenged, and in more recent years scholarship on the spatial dynamics of family formation has been renewed (see, for example, Cooke, 2008; Courgeau, 1985; Halfacree and Boyle, 1993). For example, demographers and population geographers have empirically demonstrated how mobility, particularly short-scale residential mobility, anticipates or occurs as a result of family formation events (Michielin and Mulder, 2008). What is of interest for my purpose here is how these movements are implicated by life course events as well as constrained by family circumstances. A consideration of residential change should not just, therefore, focus on the act of movement, but also on how other (im)mobilities are revealed and resolved through these movements.

Moving house

Writing in the 1950s, Peter Rossi used a family life-cycle approach to analyse migration behaviour in his book, *Why Families Move*. Rossi's conceptualisation of the relationship between mobility and family was based around housing needs: 'mobility is the mechanism by which a family's housing is brought into adjustment to its housing needs' (1956: 226). For Rossi, the main factor that affects housing needs is household size; hence at times in the family life cycle, when household size is changing rapidly, the 'household' will adjust to its changing needs through migration. According to Rossi, 'the family during this early stage typically moves from smaller to larger dwellings, from mobile "familyless" areas to areas where family living is the typical pattern of household existence' (Ibid.: 226). At the 'other end' of the life cycle, Rossi suggests that the impetus to move is more diluted, as while children leaving home and eventually the death of a partner reduce the spatial requirements of the household, it is easier to adjust to a surplus of space compared to a shortage of space. Other stages of the family life cycle are subject to different constraints, for example families with older children will be more concerned about the exterior environment and the provision of local schools and safe areas to play in. Upward social mobility (and presumably downward mobility as well) is an additional motivation for mobility, as moving to a new house is a way of expressing a family's social aspirations (or is in response to declining household income).

Rossi's account of why families move, and his coupling of mobility and family life course have a certain epistemological appeal, and would surely accord with many personal experiences of family mobility. This approach is too simplistic. First, the theorisation of family life cycle, while apposite in the 1950s, has been replaced by a less structured approach to family that emphasises dynamics and diversity rather than cycle. Second, in this framework, mobility is the outcome of changes in family and not a co-constituent; we do not get a sense of how family life and intimate relations are effectively shaped and formed through mobility. Though Rossi recognises how families utilise mobility strategies to meet aspirations about quality of life and reflect their social status, mobility is a tool rather than a practice, and thus resembles earlier visions of mobility as instrumental or about getting from A to B.

While Rossi's framework is clearly limited, his key contribution of confirming that there are times in family life when residential change is promoted and others when it is suppressed underscores an essential understanding of family life, which is that residential change can both enhance and unsettle family life. This is clearly evident if we consider the interplay between residential change and fertility. First, as Rossi points out, fertility, especially the anticipation of starting a family, is often an important reason for residential change associated with small-scale moves. Thus on small geographical scales, the relationship between anticipated fertility and household relocation can be statistically confirmed. The onset of a relationship clearly provides opportunities for mobility as couples move in together either prior to or as result of marriage. Researchers have been able to make use of longitudinal data to demonstrate the theoretical model of mobility occurring in anticipation of marriage and fertility, though the exact patterning is quite complex (Clark and Davies Withers, 2009; Michielin and Mulder, 2008). Michielin and Mulder's analysis of retrospective Dutch data demonstrates that residential mobility is more likely in the months immediately preceding marriage (and childbirth) and is suppressed after these events. Likewise, Kulu's (2008) analysis of Austrian event-history data found an increased likelihood of individual movement to rural and small urban destinations following a first conception, and this increased likelihood of moving locally was also found in relation to second conceptions, though migration over greater distances was suppressed following second or third births.

This relationship between fertility and mobility is also observable at an aggregate level, as observed by the distribution of the propensity to move by age. Infants and toddlers are the most 'mobile' of any age group under the age of 16; after these early years the risk of moving reduces dramatically. Moreover, this distinctive age pattern of mobility is relatively robust and is replicated at different geographical scales (Stillwell et al., 1996). Yet the relationship between mobility and fertility is likely to be more complex. As Clark and Withers Davies remark, 'births seem to trigger moves, but there is inconsistent evidence on the outcome of this family change' (2009: 306). One reason for this complexity is that family formation processes and family structure are more varied than is often assumed in migration studies. In addition, housing trajectories are also potentially becoming more complex, or at least less 'predictable and normative' (Ibid.: 309). The interplay between fertility and mobility is conditional on other factors, for example young couples are more likely to display fertility-related mobility than are older couples (and the likelihood of conceiving is greater in younger couples), while families with one labour force participant are more mobile than dual-worker households. The kinds of decisions that couples are making about fertility and mobility are therefore highly circumscribed by other factors, in particular labour force commitments, availability of housing and proximity to other family members, especially grandparents, who are increasingly making a vital contribution to looking after children while parents work. Families with young children may position themselves in a local housing market (those who can afford to), and in a UK context proximity to 'good' schools is also important (again, for those who can afford to move in this way). Locality is strategic to maximising the economic and social welfare of the family and the educational opportunities for children, and thus mobility decisions about where to move to have to take into account not just current needs, but also future opportunities. In the UK context in particular, a fixation on housing and education as investments has not only created a housing-price bubble, but one that varies by region and locality. Housing price variations depend on a subtle interplay of subjective judgement of value and proximity to amenities (schools often playing an important part). While obsessions with house prices and school catchment areas are part of the zeitgeist of twenty-first century urban life in the United Kingdom, mobility as a strategy for securing human capital advantage is not just a practice of late modernity. Klein's (2011) analysis of family migration in nineteenth-century Bohemia established that rural-to-urban migrations were influenced by aspirations to engage in human capital investment. The assumption of individual advancement through collective family mobility reveals the dynamic nature of family as both immanent and transcendent; family can be orientated towards both individual advancement and collective benefits simultaneously. The outcomes of strategic family movements are not just restricted to individual and collective goals, but also shape the communities within which this movement takes place. The unevenness of family migration is implicit in the creation of irregular family geographies and the formation of 'family-absent' and 'family-dominant' neighbourhoods (Smith, 2011). There is therefore a complex synchronicity between fertility, education and labour-force participation mobility, and we cannot assume that families move through a cyclical process in the way that Rossi, and more recent demographic analysis, suggest.

There is, though, an intriguing paradox about the relationship between mobility and having children. One the one hand, mobility is a strategy that many parents use to maximise children's current and future prosperity, yet at the same time mobility is popularly portrayed as undermining childhood (Holdsworth, 2013). Moving too frequently may be damaging for children, as it not only interferes with their schooling, but can potentially restrict their friendship groups as well as their sense of 'home'. Having children is therefore ultimately equated with putting down 'roots'. This ongoing tension between opposing opportunities of moving and staying put is difficult to capture in quantitative longitudinal analysis, and the demographic literature on family mobility has not been able to capture this dimension; so that literature on family mobility can be rather dry. The unfolding of families on the move is not one of moments of displacement followed by periods of consolidation, as these are oppositions that do not cancel each other out, but create the potential for each other instead. This dialectic is revealed in family narratives of mobility. In Pahl's classic study of managers and their wives carried out between 1965 and 1967, the difficulties of moving as children grow up was a recurrent theme. Both mothers and fathers interviewed in the study appreciated the importance of providing a stable and fixed location for their children. In addition, while mobility was regarded as essential for promoting husbands' careers, there becomes a time, as one respondent to Pahl's questionnaire describes, when mobility stops, which is when a 'child has reached the age where roots are required'. Parents were therefore expected to respond to changing needs within the family as children grew up and to modify their own mobility aspirations in accordance with this. Parents who did not follow the expected pattern of 'settling down' in order to provide a 'stable' and 'settled' family life were accused of putting their own needs before those of their children. One particularly intriguing aspect of Pahl's research was that some of his respondents were known to each other, thus the narratives of family mobility developed in the interviews did not just reflect personal experiences, but also included observations of other couples in the study. For example, one manager in Pahl's study discusses the circumstances of another participant in the research who had moved his family when his children were in their late teens. The manager described his friend's behaviour as selfish, as his family had not wanted to move at the time, and stated that he 'had scarred all his family by his moves, particularly his eldest child – he has sacrificed all to his promotions' (Pahl and Pahl, 1965–67). The impact on his friend's family of moving when some members of the family did not want to was that the family was split up, as the eldest teenage daughter remained in the north west of England and did not relocate with her family.

Similar anxieties are repeated for children's mobilities in other contexts, for example for children of asylum seekers and those from travelling communities, for whom there is an assumption that frequent movement over distance is equated with disruption in education, the benefits of which may depend on children staying in the same place. Interestingly, analysis of the relationship between children's recurrent mobility and educational attainment demonstrates that the relationship is context specific (Strand and Demie, 2007). While there is a correlation between mobility and educational attainment for English schoolchildren at age 11, this relationship is not found if contextual information on children's background and their earlier educational achievement are controlled for. However, this does not mean that the relationship between mobility and educational attainment is neutral, but rather that it depends on the reason for mobility. Children with low earlier-educational attainment and those for whom English is not the language spoken at home do experience lower educational attainment associated with mobility. Outside the United Kingdom, the impact of migration on children's schooling in low-income countries has been well documented (see, for example, Hashim and Thorsen, 2011). Yet this research also unsettles normative expectations about children's migration and its complexity, and it is a theme which I consider in more detail in Chapter 5.

Family migration, gender and employment

The complexity of family mobility decisions reveals the limitations of the democratic family and, in particular, the tension between individual and more collective aspirations. It is not just the needs of children that are implicated by residential moves. While residential changes in response to childbirth and housing needs are usually restricted to short-term moves, long-term moves are mostly prompted by job- and education-related factors (Détang-Dessendre and Molho, 1999; Kulu and Billari, 2004; Wagner, 1990). As explored by population geographers, these types of long-term moves are often in response to *individual* aspirations, as the participant in Pahl's research describes above in relation to his friend, and as such the implications for family members are potentially more muted. However, there is considerable interest in how long-distance family migration exposes inherent gender practices within families and the persistence of gendered ideologies. This focus on gender dimensions challenges dominant assumptions of the human capital approach to migration, which are that migration will maximise the economic potential of the household and that mobility practices have positive impacts on family and household welfare. In contrast, research that has sought to unpack the gender dimensions of family migration as related to employment challenges the simplicity of the human capital thesis and demonstrates the complexity of migration decisions and how they relate to family life. The mainstream approach to family migration and employment assumes that the decision to move is essentially an individual one that it is taken to advance the career path of one family member, and as such other family members may lose out as a result of the relocation. In particular, women's status may be threatened by migration.

There is now an extensive literature on the impact of couple migration on women's employment and income, known as the 'trailing wife' phenomenon (for example, Boyle et al., 2001, 2003; Mulder and Van Ham, 2005; Clark and Huang, 2006). These studies demonstrate how women are more likely to experience downward occupational mobility as a result of migration. Thus research on couple migration has foregrounded the importance of gender for migration decisions (Halfacree, 2004). Orientation to gender roles influences whether a couple will migrate or not, as gender roles shape how individuals prioritise their options and decisions. Thus mobility is suppressed in dual-career households in contrast to sole-breadwinner households (this observation is certainly not new to sociology of family; Parsons' structural functionalist theorisation of the nuclear family and its incorporation of distinctive gendered roles identified the nuclear family with a male breadwinner as the most mobile and thus best suited to modern capitalism). If couples with dual employment do migrate, then one member will usually experience a downward shift in occupation or, at best, a sideways move (a tied mover or trailing spouse, see Green and Canny, 2003). If the couple do not move, then one partner's occupational ambitions may also be thwarted (the tied stayer). Identifying the downward shifts of mobility is clearly easier than ascertaining immobility, and quantitative research in both the United Kingdom and the United States illustrates the weakened position of mobile-partnered women with dependent children, as opposed to those who do not move. Boyle et al.'s (2001) analysis of 1991 Census data for Great Britain illustrates that women who have moved long distances with a partner in the last year and who have dependent children have the highest inactivity rate compared to women who have either stayed put or who have moved a short distance and who also have childcare commitments. This literature also demonstrates the persistence of gendered practices, as the finding that women lose out remains consistent in different contexts (Cook et al., 2009).

While research on the impact of mobility on family structure and circumstances reveals the importance of mobility for family structure, it falls short of providing a more nuanced understanding of the interrelation between mobility and family; rather, it reinforces the view that family structure and mobility are counter-opposed: we have to work to maintain family life despite mobility (see, for example,

Schneider and Miel, 2009). The trailing spouse phenomenon presumes an individualised understanding of mobility; family mobility takes place in order to promote the individual career of one member of the household, and as such the other member suffers, thus reinforcing the expectation that mobility undermines family and intimacy.

Another shortcoming of the trailing spouse approach is that it potentially overemphasises gender as the main nexus of power and inequality in families. As discussed above, concern for children's welfare is also a factor to consider in family migration decisions, yet children do not always have the option to influence these decisions; rather, the assumption that moving is bad for children or something they do not want to do is usually made on behalf of children (Ackers, 2000; Bushin, 2009). Moreover, the main focus in family migration literature is the couple with or without children, and this emphasis on the dyadic couple essentially ignores the complexity of family diversity. To reduce 'family mobility' to studies of couple mobility presents a limited view of what family 'ought' to be. The experiences of older relatives moving closer to adult children or lone parents moving closer to their own parents are not considered as part of the 'family migration' phenomenon. Population geographers are alert to the magnitude of the scale of family diversity, for example Cooke's (2008) observation that all migration is 'family migration' recognises the limitations of fixating on married couples and their employment needs. But this also poses considerable challenges to empirical research. Residential changes that occur in response to or in anticipation of marriage, childbirth or employment are generally relatively easy to identify in quantitative longitudinal surveys, as are employment changes in response to migration. Extending the remit of family migration to consider more dynamic forms of both family and mobility is clearly a challenge to empirical research, particularly quantitative analysis.

The really significant challenge in developing a mobilities approach to family practices is not just to consider the significance of residential change for family structure and practices (and the interplay between the two) or how a 'stable' family life is maintained by hyper mobility and embedded ties – but also to address the fact that family life itself is inherently mobile and that mobility is not just about moving apart or together, but that the act of mobility is an essential family practice. Thus to develop a sustained challenge to the sedentarist perspective on family, it is important to consider family practices through mobility. In order to respond to and extend Cooke's challenge for 'family' migration, migration and mobility should not just be approached as being an outcome of life course events, but a way of managing relationships and connections. Essentially, what I am arguing here is that family practices are not bounded by fixed geographical or temporal limits; we need to move away from the idea of the essential quality of family life being rooted in one particular place – or moving between fixed and defined residences – to consider more frequent mobilities, which, in many cases are circular, repetitive and often mundane.

Intra-family mobility

One of the missing factors in the family migration puzzle is the role of other family members and networks. The wider familial and intimate context of mobility decisions is not just dictated by a couple in isolation, but rather emerges as a complex interweaving of other family demands – especially those of children and (older) parents. For example, Bailey et al. (2004) suggest that returning to live nearer parents is an important reason for moving that is not captured from a human capital perspective. Moreover, as highlighted in the brief discussion of fertility, not moving emerges as a decision that is just as important as moving. In fact the decision to move or stay is not one that can, in reality, simply be modelled as a dichotomous relationship, as often decisions to stay put are dependent on being able to access other forms of mobility; in particular, complex commuting patterns are increasingly supporting apparently 'static' families (Green, 1997). The focus on individual life course tends to highlight mobility that is associated with changes in family/intimate relations, but clearly it is far too simplistic to treat family as a static setting in between these events. Rather, moving house can reveal tensions between individual aspirations and those of other family members, and is not neutral for intra-familial relations. I have already discussed these tensions with reference to having children and putting down roots – the need for stability in family life does not always accord with other family members' aspirations or needs. However, this focus on residential change is essentially sedentarist because it highlights the complexity and difficulty of residential change and valorises immobility as the 'normal' status of family life. Notwithstanding the finding that women lose out in terms of occupation status through family mobility, what an analysis of the family migration literature reveals is how the emergence of dual-career families is restructuring mobility away from its conceptualisation as a fixed movement between two localities. Families that do not move, that is, change residential location, should not necessary be classed as immobile, as increasingly this residential immobility and ideal of static and 'stable' family life is sustained by complex patterns of daily or weekly circular mobility.

Travel to work and home/life balance

The daily travel to work is an unremarkable, but essential, mobility. Commuting takes on different spatial and temporal forms: from those who work *from* home to weekly commuters across continents, the dislocation between home and work is a persistent feature of human societies. In contemporary societies, the massive movement of people between home and work is often only considered when these systems fail to work and the complexity and interconnectivity of everyday life is exposed in full. The figure of the commuter is often depicted as an isolated individual, usually suited, male, middle class and white, trying to protect his own personal space in the confines of an overcrowded rail carriage or stuck in traffic congestion. In contrast, Iris Marion Young (2000) remarks how her own daily journey might be considered a very private and individualised one, but in travelling she is dependent not only on those who keep the transport system operational, but on others who use it. Traffic congestion is recognised as one of the banes of contemporary living; it would be far easier if travel was an essentially individual act, but the journey to work connects us, not only to home and work, but to other travellers. As I discussed earlier, when these intricate systems break down, which is usually associated with freak events, particular climatic ones, our reliance on just being able to travel and how our individual travel needs are dependent on others are revealed.

Commuting is usually considered to be an economic practice more than a family practice. For example, we usually refer to the 'journey to work' rather than the journey from/to home. Yet these daily/weekly journeys connect both home and work, and in doing so are shaped by practices at both home and work. The need to recognise the interconnectivity between home and work is not a new argument in social geography. In the 1980s Hanson and Pratt's seminal work argued that home and work cannot be treated as separate spheres, rather they are conceptualised as competing for the same time demands of family members, leading to both a policy and an academic interest in how individuals juggle family life. One of the most conceptually appealing geographical studies of everyday mobility is Hägerstrand's time–space geography (1970). These paths reveal how individuals are able to multitask, and outline the detailed individual day-paths and week-paths that individuals develop in order to sustain disparate roles. These paths are not constructed in a vacuum, but social identities are reproduced through daily commuting patterns. Statistics of daily community patterns reveal that women travel shorter distances (if measured by time or distance) and higher earners travel longer ones. Politicians recognise that appealing to the work/life balance can be an effective policy discourse, as many families 'struggle' to make this balance work. Discourse around work/life balance, however, also reinforces the ideal that, in a perfect world, work and home *should* be balanced, while in reality this balance does not exist (Holmes, 2004). Moreover, achieving this balance is theorised as an individualised process; it is up to women and men in their everyday lives to make this 'balance' work, thus negating how other structuring forces make achieving this balance an unobtainable goal. In particular it falls on women to negotiate the demands of work and home; consequently, it is not surprising to find that women's travel to work patterns are distinctive from men's (see Law, 1999).

In recognising the context within which commuting takes place – that it is not simply determined by individual choice – we can extend this approach to consider how classed and gendered practices create the space in which they occur. These practices have emerged over time. At the beginning of the nineteenth century, men's status was defined through engagement in the public space outside the home. Home was a place to journey from and return to, and these comings and goings framed the temporality of life within the home: men's departure from and return to the home were ritually marked and framed the timings of home-based activities (Walsh, 2009). In contrast, for women home was a place of work and opportunities to travel outside the home were more constrained. This is not to suggest that women had no freedom, but their freedom was limited and was in deference to their role within the home. This gendered difference in everyday mobilities to and from home not only shaped differential experiences of home, but had profound impacts on communities, particularly in the newly created suburbs on the outskirts of urban conurbations, to which the middle class retreated to create and endorse privatised home life. The impact of gendered mobility practices on neighbourhoods has been recorded in oral history accounts of family and community. Thompson's influential study of Edwardians included the oral history of Katherine Chorley, who had grown up in Alderley Edge, a commuter town on the outskirts of Manchester. Katherine remembered how the differential mobility of men and women impacted on daily life there. She describes how, after the 9.18 a.m. train had departed to Manchester,

> the Edge became exclusively female. You never saw a man on the hill roads unless it were the doctor or the plumber and you never saw a man in anyone's home except the gardener or the coachman.
>
> (Thompson, 1992: 29)

The demarcated pattern of mobility described by Katherine Chorley in Edwardian Alderley Edge no longer applies to urban or suburban space. Home and work are now interlinked in more complex ways following changes in women's employment in the latter half of the twentieth century. Her account, though, also masks the complexity of gender, work and mobility relations. Even in places such as Alderley Edge, women have always worked, as the well-off middle classes were supported by domestic workers. Young working-class women were expected to leave home and find work as domestic workers, yet their experiences (and those of other working-class women who strategised to support their families) are often ignored in the accounts of women's employment. Alderley Edge was exclusively female during the daytime because of the patterns of men's as well as women's employment. However, while working-class women continued to find work in immediate localities, the partners of the middle-class men in Alderley Edge had a very different employment pattern. The rise of the middle-class dual-career family has intrigued geographers because of the complexity of making sense of more than one commuting pattern and, in particular, how this depends on a complex hyper mobility of all family members, that is, adults going to work, children going to school and the mobility of home-help and other bought-in services.

Reconciling mobility and immobility

Anne Green's (1997) analysis of dual-career families foregrounds the complexity of the interplay between mobility and career decisions, and challenges the assumption that career advancement decisions would be automatically prioritised over other considerations. Even though the majority of households that Green interviewed identified a lead 'career', and in most cases this was the man's, this did not preclude couples employing considerable care and thought in seeking to develop mobility strategies that could maximise benefits to both individuals and households. One way of doing this was to establish a fixed residence that maximised mobility (for example, through access to rail or road networks to more than one urban conurbation). Moreover, this fixed residence was often associated with the ideal of living in the countryside, or at least a semi-rural environment, and the 'freedom' that this afforded to family members. Thus Green's account of the mobility decisions of 'privileged' dual-career households illustrates how the permanency of residence and the importance put on the 'ideal' residence could only be achieved through flexibility in employment and a daily ultra mobility of working partners who became increasingly tolerant of long-distance commuting (see also van der Klis and Karsten, 2009; van der Klis and Mulder, 2008). These complex, mobile lives therefore revolve around a fixed, permanent base. Writing in 1997, Green makes the pertinent observation that the environmental impact of this individualised ultra mobility and high level of dependence on automobility and access to road networks was ignored by respondents. But the very practices that sustained family life in the semi-rural localities threatened the rural idyll that the couples sought to aspire to in their housing decisions.

Hyper mobility is one solution to reconciling work and family, though it is by no means the only one. An alternative approach is to fold work and home into the same space. The rise of home-located production supported by communication technology is a notable trend in industrialised countries, with recent estimates for the United Kingdom suggesting that just over one in ten workers are based at home. Yet this technology-facilitated rise in home working masks other established practices, in particular that home working can also be poorly paid and gendered (Felstead and Jewson, 2000). Though home working is often regarded as an optimum way of reconciling the work/life balance and forgoing the need for mobility between distinctive locations, the implications of this folding of public and private space are rarely considered. Seymour's (2007) account of the single location workplace, using family-run hotels, pubs and boarding houses as exemplars is a notable exception. As Seymour remarks, the blending between work and home is particular poignant, as the ideology of these establishments is often about creating a home from home for their guests. Seymour describes the layering of different practices within the homes; that families were both resistant and flexible in how they dealt with the intrusion of business into 'private' family life.

Empirical case studies of home workers foreground other mobilities that are ignored in conventional accounts of family mobility organised around commuting to work, that is, mobility into the home, which may include family and non-family members. As I discussed in the previous chapter, domestic service provided an important conduit for youth mobility until the early-twentieth century, and while it has become more marginalised and hidden in more recent years, employment within the home remains an importance nexus for the creation and persistence of gendered class relations (McDowell, 2006). The hyper-mobility practices of dual-career families not only sustain the apparent immobility of domestic forms, but in turn are sustained by a counter-mobility of service, predominantly that of women in domestic service. Contemporary forms of commodified care and service do have a distinctive mobility compared to early formulations in that these are less likely to be provided within the home, particularly in the case of childcare. Cleaning services are often outsourced through agencies, rather than by the employment of a regular home help or live-in domestic service. For McDowell and her colleagues (2006), this respatialisation of care is part of the social speeding-up of family and work lives, with women's work within the home supplemented by the provision of care at fixed localities outside the home; this commodification of care is recognised as having more demands on time and mobility. The problems faced by women in McDowell et al.'s study, particularly in London, were mostly to do with the inflexibility of a transport system designed

around the assumption of commuting to work that did not necessarily fit with other mobility demands such as taking a child to
nursery. Mobility is therefore both a facilitator and a barrier to care
(Barker, 2011).

However, this concern with the practicalities of increasingly connected lives is still very much located within a sedentarist paradigm:
getting from A to B, particularly with a small child in tow or having to
travel between successive cleaning or caring jobs, is a barrier to activities and not part of these activities. Ferguson's (2009) analysis of the
mobile practices of social workers describes how cars are more than
just a means of travelling between clients, echoing Laurier's (2004)
observations that they are also a location within which work is done
(for example, form filling) and a means of taking clients to and from
new residences, including removing vulnerable children from home
and taking them into care. The car, as Ferguson describes it, has been
essential to the practice of social care, not only in facilitating work,
but in providing a space for therapeutic encounters. As Ferguson succinctly states, to understand the role of the car in social work is to
recognise it as 'a "fluid container" for the processing of personal trou-
bles, emotion and key life changes, which, when used skilfully, assists
vulnerable people in making healing journeys' (2009: 277). I shall
return to this theme in the penultimate chapter on intimate spaces,
but here in the context of understanding mobilites around work,
Ferguson's approach highlights the importance of mobility itself, in
that mobility not only sustains employment and care and eases the
apparent tension between the two, but can also provide spaces for
care. Travelling within the duties of a working day or shift, including
commuting to and from work, is more than about getting from A to
B or even a continuation of work, but it can provide an added value
to the assumed fixed and static practices of employment. Edensor
(2008) develops this narrative of the therapeutic potential of commuting in discussing how time to talk to oneself, listen to the radio
and enjoy the experience of driving suggests a different way of experiencing commuting than repetitive boredom driven by the desire to
get to one's destination as quickly as possible. Commuting is therefore both individual and collective; it is about connecting different
spheres, but this act of connection is not neutral, and this time of
liminal suspension between work and home can be a very private
space.

A final consideration of 'commuting' should also consider employment that entails frequent and extended absences, for example military families, workers in offshore locations or industrial contractors. Despite the fact that these forms of employment are by no means new, the experiences of these families is largely absent from the family practices or migration literature. These experiences are mostly celebrated for the immobile structures that they leave behind, for example navvies and railwaymen of the nineteenth century are remembered through the canals and railways that facilitated the mobility of labour and goods but the impact on their families is less considered (Walsh, 2009). For military families, the emphasis is very much on the psychosocial aspect of the deployment of family members on active service away from home (see, for example, Park, 2011). The conventional view is 'that when one person joins, the whole family serves' (Park, 2011), and this is apposite during peace as well as during conflict. For example, families often have to cope with current relocations, as families are moved around military camps. Relocation can be a positive experience, providing children in particular with opportunities to meet new friends, and for some children it is identified with greater independence and maturity (Ibid.). While the military might be regarded as a special case of extended family absence, other experiences of work-related absences are even more muted in the literature.

Achieving immobility is therefore an active process and is sustained by differential mobility practices. The desire for stability and 'rootedness' cannot be equated with the absence of movement, but rather with how mobility practices can come together to sustain immobility.

Conclusion

Moving home is a significant event in contemporary modern societies. In fact, in countries such as the United Kingdom, with a high percentage of owner occupancy, buying and selling 'family' homes is somewhat of an obsession, and moving house is an important part of family life. While, as I discussed in the previous chapter, residential change is implicit in family/partnership formation and dissolution, families also move together, and these residential changes can have different impacts on family members. However, the key argument that I have developed in this chapter is the need for caution in overstating the dichotomy between moving and staying put, as decisions to move are often mediated by other mobility decisions, for example daily commuting patterns and proximity to family and other relatives. In order to develop this more integrated approach to family mobility, it is necessary to interweave family migration with other less-fixed forms of family mobility (for example, daily commuting) as part of the same process. A key consideration is how mobility reveals the inherent quality of intimate relations, particularly how they are structured by power relations; specifically, the nexus of gender and age are often implicated through mobility decisions and practices. Mobility can therefore reveal the limitations to more egalitarian forms of relationships as well as offering a way of accommodating different individual trajectories within a family setting. Families on the move are very often uneven, combining different requirements for stasis and mobility between family members. Sometimes mobilities are forced upon others, such as the trailing spouse, and at other times they are denied, such as when the modification of individual career paths is prioritised over the needs of other family members. The intricacy of resolving work and family balances takes different spatial forms. These might include relocation, complex daily or weekly commuting, bringing work into the home or outsourcing care.

This account of families on the move has focused on two collective practices – moving house and daily mobilities to and from home – and how these are interconnected. In the following chapter this theme is developed through consideration of more varied forms of collective mobility that are less directional and more nomadic and non-linear.

5
Families on the Move II: Nomadic, Non-Linear and Children's Mobilities

There is clearly more to family mobilities than residential moves and commuting, though academic research on family mobility has developed a bias towards themes that are intrinsically about the relationship between family and the economy (Morgan, 1996). Thus residential moves are often, though not always, theorised as a mechanism for job advancement; from Colin Bell's accounts in the 1960s of middle-class spiralists to more recent European Union-funded projects that focus on the difficulties of reconciling job mobility and family life (Schneider and Collet, 2009; Schneider and Meil, 2008), there is a tendency to promote the economic functionality of family life and the hegemony of the dyadic couple. Accounts of family mobility are often too reliant on the observation of permanent moves and the couple as the main nexus of intimate relations. The intricacies of intimate and family life can be hidden in accounts that only consider mobility in the context of employment. Family mobility cannot, though, be reduced to considering a dyadic reading of family, but it entails a complex and intricate meshing of family life that involves both other family members (for example, parents/grandparents) and significant others (for example, friends, including children's social networks). Family mobility does not fall into a neat compartmentalisation between long-term migrations that infer residential change and other short- or long-distance movements such as daily/weekly commuting practices. Both of these practices assume that families are located in one particular place and that mobility involves either a change in residence or individual movements to and from this fixed residence. Yet families on the move include more incidental and radial forms of mobility, temporary relocations such as holidays and more prolonged, or seasonal, nomadic forms. This suggests a shift from linear forms of mobility to more non-linear movements. Moreover, discussions of family mobility should not be wholly inward looking, as this assumes a rather limited interpretation of family and falls short of the more diverse and active reading of family practices. These intricacies relate to the relevance of mobilities of all family members within a complex spatial geometry and how people interact with others both in their immediate vicinity and further afield.

In this chapter, I extend the discussion of families on the move beyond the relationship between family and work by discussing three case studies of distinct, but interrelated, mobility themes: children's mobility, nomadic mobilities and the non-linear mobilities of family support and conviviality. These three case studies of family mobility are considered to highlight the variability of movement with reference to the subject of mobility (such as a shift away from an adultist perspective), the direction and permanency of mobility and mobilities associated with obligation rather than choice. The case studies also highlight the fragility of grand narratives of social change relating to family and mobility. In both public and academic contexts, the need to make sense of the complexity of family mobility practices is associated with broad generalisations about the direction of social change, for example with reference to declining independent mobility, a decline in propinquity and the need to maintain relations over distance. The inherent quality of non-linear mobility is its variability, though, and as such the direction of social change is cyclical rather than linear.

Children's mobility

The previous discussion of both family relocation and commuting spilled over into consideration of children, though children remained the object of these mobility practices. The need to get location 'right' for children and to provide stability *and* access to quality schools is an important theme for family relocation, while commuting is increasingly having to take on board children's mobility to day care or school. Yet these debates are still very much adultist in orientation. For example, concern about the school run is often taken from the perspective of adults. School runs are held up as causing congestion for others and impeding the economically driven mobility of adults; moral panics around children's increasingly sedentary lives guide how adults make choices about children's mobility.

Independent mobility

Children's mobility patterns have received considerable attention from researchers in recent years (Barker et al., 2009; Holdsworth, 2013; Holt and Costello, 2011; Ní Laoire et al., 2010; White et al., 2011). This has been influenced by the emergence of the 'new sociological studies' of childhood that have sought to emphasise children's capacity for agency and subjectivity, rather than depicting them as passive objects to whom the adults' world is a separate and discrete sphere (Holloway and Valentine, 2000; Matthews and Limb, 1999; Skelton, 2009). This growing interest in the study of childhood has, though, generated a tension between how researchers identify the importance of childhood as a particular age period, distinctive from adult life, and as such how they have sought to carry out research about children from their own perceptive. An alternative, though not necessarily competing, paradigm (though, see Hopkins and Pain, 2007, and Horton and Kraftl, 2008, for a discussion of this debate) has been sought to reveal the relationships between children and others from the perspective of intergenerationality. Within both paradigms, the significance of mobility is clearly recognised. Studies of childhood have generated an extensive scholarship on children's mobilities and spatiality and a mapping of children's 'independent mobility' and how different spaces are used and interpreted by children (see, for example, Barker et al., 2009; Mikkelsen and Christensen, 2009), including their use of public spaces and the different ways that children appropriate space, particularly with regard to play and education. Underlying much of this scholarship are assumptions about the importance of childhood away from adults' gaze and about how children's 'freedom' has been constrained in many contemporary societies as parents become more risk averse. There is a considerable amount of hand-wringing among commentators alarmed at how the increasingly sedentary lives of children are damaging their health, well-being and development. As Sibley (1995a) succinctly summarises, the overall trend of contemporary childhood is one that is becoming increasingly home centred.

As a counterpoint to this, emerging interest in the fluidity and mobility of young people's lives has sought to unravel children's appropriation of space and how they value and define their own mobility. An underlying narrative here is concerned with the meaning and significance of independent mobility, with children needing to learn to take risks on their own away from home and with how these kinds of engagement stimulate children's development. Commentators on contemporary childhood have identified a 'worrying' trend towards sedentary childhoods that are a product of 'toxic' (Palmer, 2006) or 'denatured' (Louv, 2005) childhoods. Palmer's writings on toxic childhood have received considerable support in the United Kingdom; in particular, two letters sent to the *Times* in September 2007 and 2008 signed by a variety of dignitaries associated in some way with children. These highlight concerns that 'toxic' childhood was caused by an overarching concern with testing at school, over-reliance on technology for entertainment and childhoods increasingly unfolding in sanitised, 'safe' places, that is, the school and home, between which children are moved, usually by car. The result of these trends, according to Palmer, was a childhood not only bereft of danger or excitement but also of normal play and socialising. She argues that children are missing out on how to negotiate risk on their own; they are losing out on social interaction skills; moreover, children are becoming more stressed as a result of an education system that emphasises testing and measuring individual children's development against a linear progression; finally, children's health is at risk, and this is particularly associated with an increase in childhood obesity through lack of exercise. Discussions of denatured childhood overlap with some of the concerns raised in the toxic childhood literature. Louv's (2005) account of denatured childhood, in particular, alludes to the significance of areas of wilderness and natural landscapes for children's development; he argues that there is a direct link between the absence of nature in children's lives and the rise in obesity, attention and other behaviour disorders and mental health problems.

The appeal of the natural world is also a common theme in children's imaginary geographies, and many classic texts in children's literature make use of a journey metaphor in wild or unfamiliar settings to explore children's development and how they learn about themselves and others. One of the more celebrated examples of this approach is Frances Hodgson Burnett's *The Secret Garden*, published in 1911, that tells the story of Mary, abandoned in her guardian's house on the edge of the North Yorkshire moors, and her crippled cousin Colin, who are befriended by the local village boy Dickon and learn about the appeal of nature through their encounter with the 'secret garden'. Both children learn not only about themselves but also about how to interact with others and bring out the affection of Colin's father and Mary's guardian. *The Secret Garden* remains a classic in children's literature, not only because of the quality of Hodgson Burnett's writing, but also for the appeal of the metaphor of nature as healing, for children as well as adults. There are other notable literary works that have interwoven children's engagement with adventure and wilderness, with adults either very much in the background, such as Arthur Ransome's *Swallows and Amazon*, or with parents and other adults appearing vaguely oppressive, for example in Richmal Crompton's *William* stories. The appeal of adventure is not just restricted to literary endeavours, but it is endorsed by organisations such as the Scout Association and the Guides Association, which continue to support young people spending time away from family at organised holidays and camps.

The appeal of the motif of escape and adventure in children's literature reflects a real tension between control and freedom. Thus the study of children's mobility does not just focus on children's practices, but also on how mobility is a site for negotiation between children and adults. For example, Barker's (2009) study on children in cars, while challenging the adultist stance of automobility research (not least because of the fact that children cannot be the car driver), explores how the car is a site for a variety of different activities, from consumption/play/homework and those that involve interaction between children and parents. It is this focus on the intergenerational potential of mobility that is most germane for my interest here. Children's mobility, whether accompanied by an adult or not, is closely linked to managing intergenerational relations. Moreover, as children grow up and move through the teenage years, mobility is one resource that they can adapt. The constant comings and goings in households with older children generate a very different experience of mobility, compared to the more constrained and regulated mobility of children at younger ages. For some families, the experience may make them feel that their home is not just being treated like a hotel, but has come to seem like a mainline rail-way terminus: it is a point of both departure and return, if only briefly. As discussed in Chapter 4 on individual mobility, these move-ments can be seen as part of the process of leaving and returning home, and as children move through the transition to adulthood, their experiences of mobility become more individualised and less collective.

Children's mobility between households

One important aspect of children's mobility is movement between different places of residence. Though, children's mobility is often conceptualised as a movement from a single point of home to outside spaces (particularly school), yet for many children mobility patterns often involve more than one family setting. Moving between differ-ent houses is relevant for children whose parents have separated, but it is also the norm for many children who are looked after by rela-tives or friends. Increasingly, the school run, particularly the journey home, involves a staging point, for example going to a grandpar-ent's house before being picked up by parents later on. Many children have their own toys and bedrooms at relatives' homes, usually grand-parents' homes, in part because they spend time there. But it is the experiences of children in post-separation families that challenge some of the normative expectations about children's mobility, and it is to these experiences that I now turn.

On Friday evenings in various pub car parks and motorway ser-vice stations, a ritual can be observed. Children arrive with one parent to be 'handed over', often with a small bag of belongings, to the parent they will spend the weekend with, returning again on a Sunday evening. These exchanges are often short and unre-markable to any passing observer, yet this ritual is an increasingly 'normal' part of many children's lives. While the handover itself might be unremarkable, what it signifies for all those involved is far from trivial. Moreover, the 'non-places' of transit in which these han-dovers occur are not just important locations for family practices, but are sites of interactions and meetings that make mobilities possible (Merriman, 2004). To return to the child in transit, for the most part the experiences of children in this arrangement are usually portrayed as damaging. Again, I turn to children's literature to consider how mobility after parental separation is portrayed. The extremely popular children's author Jacqueline Wilson in her depiction of children's experiences of parental divorce in the *Suitcase Kid* (1992), while sympathetic to her protagonist Andrea, describes her coming to terms with the situation as something that she has to do on her own, accompanied only by her toy rabbit Radish. Radish is her constant companion as she moves between her parents' houses and has to learn to deal with her parents' decision to split up and the new family arrangements post-divorce. Both parents form new relationships, and Andrea's experiences are of the transition from a stable, secure family (symbolised by the home with the mulberry tree in the front garden) to messy and difficult family arrangements. While Andrea does learn to come to terms with her parents' separation, her sense of yearning for the past frames her journey to becoming, and accepting being, a 'suitcase kid'. Echoing the narrative of *The Secret Garden*, Andrea comes to terms with her new mobile life though imaginative play with Radish in another garden with a mulberry tree and is befriended by the elderly couple who live there. Wilson's portrayal of a child moving between two dysfunctional homes with just a suitcase and a toy rabbit underscores a normative expectation that children *should not* be on the move. Children need the kind of rooted, grounded family life that will support them eventually through the transition to adulthood.

Wilson's account of the *Suitcase Kid* offers a role model for children going through similar experiences as well as providing an understanding for children who have not experienced parental divorce but who need to understand the experiences of friends who have to adapt to changing family situations. The overarching theme, though, is that children should not be expected to be constantly on the move and that it is not sufficient to expect children to adapt to parents' changing needs and priorities. The importance of situating children's needs as the most important entitlement has, however, been effectively integrated into the legal process of divorce and separation. Smart and Neale's (1999) detailed account of post-separation parenting effectively demonstrates why the 1989 Children Act makes it a priority to put a child's needs first. This is associated with ensuring that shared parental responsibility is maintained during and after separation. The danger of not putting children's needs first is that, as in the case of Andrea, children are objectified by the process and treated as possessions that can be argued about – and divided – between parents.

How parents can maintain the best interests of the child is far from clear. It requires negotiation and input from all involved. However, it usually remains the case that it is children who move between different residences (as in Andrea's case), and not parents who are mobile. As such, the image of the suitcase kid has come to represent contemporary relationship breakdown rather than children abandoned by parents. Clearly, the experiences of children in post-separation families will be very different: some will see very little (if any) of one parent, while others will follow the kind of nomadic lifestyle experienced by Andrea. In between these two extremes of solo parenting and shared parenting, many children will have different arrangements for seeing parents, ranging from every other weekend and once a week (usually Wednesdays, which has led to another ritual of contemporary family life of the Wednesday night trip to the pizza restaurant for dad and the kids) to only being able to see the non-resident parent during school holidays. Others will have supervised contact arranged at contact centres with no opportunity for overnight visits. The complexity of arrangements that actually exist is a result of individual circumstances that depend on the interplay within the relationship between separated parents as well as between children and parents and parents' commitment to new families, kin and work. Clearly, practices of post-separation parenting have evolved in the post-Children's Act era, during which, as Smart and Neale (1999) have described so appositely, parents have had to 'refashion parenthood' without any normative blueprint. However, to have such a normative blueprint would not be sensible, as it is impossible to stipulate what kinds of arrangements should be in place without reference to parental circumstances. In England and Wales, policy interventions that have sought to oppose a one-size-fits-all solution have ended in failure: the intervention of the Child Support Agency into the calculation and collection of child maintenance is a case in point (Jones and Perrin, 2009).

For many – but not all – children in post-separation families, some form of mobility between different homes will be a core factor in maintaining relationships with both parents. While the focus of my interest here is children's mobility between parental homes, there are other residential mobilities that might be equally important.

In particular, spending time with grandparents is a common practice for many children, regardless of parents' relationship status. Hence the kinds of residential mobilities that children are engaged in might well be more complex than simply moving between two homes, and they might involve other key places such as the homes of family members and friends. For children who move regularly between parental homes, as described above, the frequency and duration of visits to both homes will be quite varied and is unlikely to stay constant over time. As children grow up and develop their own friendship networks, mobility between parental homes might impede this, and then their mobility patterns between parental homes might change. Likewise, parents' lives are not on hold: parents might form new relationships and new families or they might want to seek out new opportunities (for example, a new job) and move away from their children. Hence mobility and flux are not only characteristic of children's daily/weekly/monthly lives, but these patterns of mobility are unlikely to remain fixed over time. There is a constant theme of balance and 'getting' it 'right'; different responsibilities and demands are negotiated through these mobility practices, though often with a sense of sacrifice on all sides. The three contradictory elements of shared parenting are, as Haugen (2010) describes, flexibility, ambiguity and rigidity. Yet Haugen goes on to argue that while we should acknowledge children's agency, we also need to be wary about placing too much responsibility on children and be aware that it is not just up to children to negotiate how these arrangements work.

Some form of mobility is required for most post-separation contact (though in some families, especially those where one parent lives a considerable distance away, it might be the parent who does the travelling rather than the children). Not surprisingly, the distance between the resident and non-resident parent is a key factor in determining how often or whether non-resident parents see their children. Parents who live close by see their children more regularly than those who live further away. However, the causality between distance and contact is not necessarily straightforward: for parents to separate, at least one parent has to move, and he/she may feel a desire to move on and move away to start a new life somewhere else. In some cases, parents may not be able to live close by; for example, they may have to move with work or have to move to a new area as they cannot afford to live closer. Moreover, it is not necessarily the parent without residence that does the 'moving away'. Parents with residence rights might choose to move closer to relatives, especially their own parents, in order to support themselves and their children. There is therefore a complex series of negotiations that underlie where parents live and how contact is maintained. Access to resources will also be essential in facilitating these kinds of movements. In the United Kingdom and the United States, so-called weekender children are often dependent on both parents' automobility, and access to transport ties is clearly essential in supporting these movements. Public transport can have a role; for example, in Germany the Deutsche Bahn's escort service 'Kids on Tour' accompanies children travelling on their own on Friday and Sunday evening, and in 2009 looked after 6229 children who were travelling alone (Schier and Proske, 2010). For parents choosing to share care, access to suitable housing in reasonably proximate neighbourhoods will be a key factor, as will be supporting two family-size homes. As such, the kinds of contact arrangements that parents can enter into is contingent on their own material circumstances. Research on post-separation children demonstrates how poverty is the most damaging aspect of post-separation life (Ní Bhrolcháin et al., 2000), and it would seem reasonable to conclude that parents with few resources will find it harder to support the kinds of hyper-mobility patterns that post-separation parenting requires.

Post-separation parenting and childhood not only reconfigure how parental responsibility can be shared between parents no longer in relationships but also challenge a view of childhood, encountered in several places in this book, that childhood is synonymous with being rooted and that children need physical stability in order to develop a 'stable' adult personality. Ann Magrit Jensen (2009) suggests a different interpretation, which is that children's mobility is essential not only to maintain relationships with significant others, who are not spatially contingent, but it might also result in children developing coping strategies that will put them at an advantage in adult life. Getting used to being on the move in a mobile world could actually be beneficial for children rather than damaging, as is often popularly portrayed. Being able to develop a dialectical understanding of the importance of both staying put and moving on could be viewed as an important learning experience. If children's mobility involves the use of different transport types, particularly public transport, children's mobility between parental homes could also be providing them with key life skills. However, it would be reasonable to assume that the extent to which we can interpret children's mobility between parental homes as beneficial will be highly contingent on individual circumstances. Contact arrangements that allow very little room for negotiation, in which children are effectively pawns moved around between houses and with little dialogue between all parties, might be less constructive than arrangements that afford more negotiation and are responsive to children's needs. Does being transported up and down a motorway on a Friday and Sunday night necessarily enrich children's appreciation of mobility, other than fostering a detailed understanding of the inconvenience of congestion? If children are to 'benefit' from acculturation to the practices of mobility, then some degree of agency and control is probably necessary.

Children may also feel disadvantaged by the burden of the expectation that they have to share their time equally between parents and that it is up to children to ensure that this happens rather than adults. As Wade and Smart (2003) describe from research with older children, this sense of responsibility of sharing co-presence did not necessarily end when children grew up, but carried forward through creating negotiations about key family events: Christmas, weddings, birthdays and so on. These kinds of events are popularly symbolised as times when families do get together and when corporeal co-presence is obligatory. There are some key family moments that are not spatially divisible.

Seasonal/nomadic family mobility

Many forms of family mobility do not radiate from one fixed point. In addition to the complexity of many children's mobilites between different localities, families are also on the move in response to both economic and seasonal conditions, such as escaping cold winters (or sometimes hot summers). Seasonal and return mobilities are hardly a recent phenomenon of family life, as both natural and social climates have long influenced human mobility. However, these rhythmical forms of mobility have for the most part been ignored by researchers of both family life and mobility and migration, despite the fact that they are a common form of mobility. For example, McHugh et al. (1995) illustrate the importance of temporary into- and out-of-state movements as well as dual residence among the elderly population in Arizona, where an estimated one quarter of the population aged 60 and over reports one of these three temporary migration practices. While acknowledging the particular context of temporary migration in a sunbelt state such as Arizona (that is, a state to which the elderly move temporarily during the winter), not all forms of temporary migration fit this 'snowbird' pattern, but rather point to the complexity of temporary mobility patterns. McHugh suggests that this dimension of mobility is one that is often lost in systematic approaches to migration that emphasise fixed location. He contends that:

> Variegated forms of spatial mobility – migration, local moves, travel, seasonal movements – are embedded in personal, family and community histories, and evolve in complex ways over the life course.
>
> (McHugh, 2000: 79)

Accounts of cyclical migration among elderly Arizonians reveal how these travellers developed connections with the communities that they moved out of in the summer and with the other mobile travellers. Thus nomadic wanderings were not necessarily associated with lack of belonging. Mullins and Tucker's study of Canadian 'snowbirds' (retirees who seasonally migrate between Canada and Florida) concluded that:

> [they] were nomadic in the sense that their social ties were primarily with the same migrants in the communities they shared at both ends of the move. Their ties were not to places but to the migrating community itself
>
> (cited in Phillipson, 2007: 329).

Nomadic mobilities do not need to be experienced with rootlessness; rather, they can be associated with an affinity to movement which can be shared with others.

One way in which these forms of nomadic mobilities have become more institutionalised is through the expansion of family holidays. Intriguingly, family holidays are missing in the literature on either mobility or family practices (see, for example, Obrador, 2012).

Mobilities literature does include extensive discussion of *tourism*, though from the perspective of the individual traveller, and family practices literature has focused predominantly on domestic settings. Yet outside academic writings, the value of family holidays is universally recognised. This is evident in more recent campaigns to promote social tourism and in the policy to enable all families and individuals to have 'time away' regardless of resources (Minnaert, 2008). From this standpoint, 'holidays are a right for all' (ibid.: 15). The advantages are that family holidays are uncontroversial: they promote well-being, improve family communication and consolidate family ties (ibid.: 14). Holidays are increasingly synonymous with family mobility, not just in relation to the summer break, but throughout the year family events are increasingly associated with getting away from home; as such, part of the travel chaos at Christmas and Easter is not just families being reunited, but families getting away from it all. The chaos that this is associated with is often contrasted with the more 'orderly' and normative chaos of the daily commute. In December 2009, when major engineering works on the north-west main line (a key rail link in the United Kingdom) overspilled into the New Year period so that commuters were affected on returning to work, the company responsible was severely criticised for the impact that this had on commuters rather than for how it might have disrupted family migration over the Christmas break. Holidays are valued, but disruption is more acceptable at holiday times than during 'normal' working hours.

An intriguing quality about the family holiday is that it symbolises family 'quality' time, which is achieved through mobility – getting away from it all, without defining what 'all' actually is. The literature on leisure mobility and tourism highlights the normalisation of long-distance travel (Edensor, 2007), while still acknowledging how access to resources differentiates who can participate in this form of 'normalised' travel: distinctions are made between and within high- and low-income countries (Frändberg, 2009). Moreover, long-distance travel is associated with maintaining relationships and geographically diverse social networks – it is not just about visiting exotic places: in fact, this form of mobility has become 'de-exoticized' (Franklin and Crang, 2001; Larsen et al., 2007). Yet accounts of contemporary mobility through tourism develop an individualised perspective, often by considering the experiences of young people taking part in leisure tourism as a form of rite of passage. There is less written about how going away as a family is important. Rather, accounts of tourist mobility tend to focus on mobility that is associated with distinct cultural experiences or with reaffirming or challenging identities. In contrast, many family holidays are not necessarily associated with developing networks but are more about a temporary displacement of the everyday. Where does this leave the family holiday and what does spending time away from home in a family context symbolise? In Löfgren's (1999) history of vacationing, family is both present and absent; while the symbolism of the holiday as a time for family togetherness is recognised in the first images in the book, 'family' holidays are treated as a particular form of vacationing associated with automobilities and camping. His reading of vacation is very much directed at the individual tourist seeking a break from both domestic and work routines:

> Going on a vacation meant taking yourself, as a tourist, to another time and space, a transformation emphasizing being outside normal life, and the routines of home and workplace. Such rituals of passage could produce the pleasant release of pressure from your back, easing the burden of everyday commitments, routines, and demands. Any activity, from repairing a roof to building a sand castle becomes nonwork. Vacation life became territorialized hedonism.
>
> (1999: 269)

Yet I argue that the 'family' holiday is more than a temporary displacement or a time when families can just 'get away from it all' – it cannot be separated from routine daily family practices. Holidays are saved for and planned for, and, through the holiday, 'normal' family life is legitimated. For example, in ethnographic research carried out by Sarah Hall on the ethics of everyday family consumption, the importance of saving up for holidays emerged as a key feature of everyday consumption. Respondents frequently talked about how their everyday spending took into account saving to go on holiday, and, moreover, that working hard in order to 'earn' a break was legitimate:

> yeah, holidays are something that are really important to us, so that's kind of, we wouldn't, I wouldn't sacrifice that at all, that's

sort of, like I'd rather go on holiday than have anything else or do anything else. I'd rather do without quite a lot, like nights out or anything, because it's quite important to us, particularly for Joseph because he works really, really hard, like he works ongoing still...so, like, for him going on holiday is, like, quite important.

For this family, holidays are not something extra but one of the most important events for family consumption, and they are prioritised over other purchases or events. From this perspective, holidays justified the hard work for the rest of the year: 50 weeks of hard work juggling work/life balance for two weeks of 'family' bliss and relaxation. Holidays have become an accepted way of reconciling family life and employment commitments. In his classic essay, 'Time and Work Discipline', the historian E. P. Thompson considers how the tension over working and holidays was enforced and resisted in the early years of industrialisation (1993). While workers in the early nineteenth century sought to protect the practices of Saint Monday (and even Tuesday) as times for intoxication and not being at work, in late modernity the justification of time off has been condensed into a more consolidated form of a couple of weeks and the occasional public holiday.

Family holidays incorporate a number of ideals of family, time and work:

- They are a valuable break from routines and allow time to be together as a family.
- Family holidays are a form of consumption, yet are not isolated from more mundane purchases. Rather, holidays are saved up for, and part of the rationale of working hard and having less family time during the year is that this is a way of affording time together on holiday.
- We reaffirm family life by breaking away from daily practices that sustain families, and there is an important recognition that one way of doing family 'properly' is by spending time away from both the spatial location of family practice and the time routines that families keep to.

However, family holidays are also popularly associated with stress and boredom, so maybe they are less conducive to reaffirming family life than we might think. In Hall's ethnographic research, discussed above, the data collected on family consumption while families were away on holiday revealed a far more prosaic experience than families believed they had. For example, one mother suggested that her family ate far more healthily when away from home, and that they had more salads and barbeques. Yet analysis of family photos and receipts collated while on holiday revealed that her family predominantly consumed packaged and prepared food away from home. Holidays are envisioned as exceptional times, even if the reality is more mundane. One of the most valuable aspects of going away is returning home to appreciate the daily practices of family life. Hence what is often celebrated or endorsed through these mobilities is not the process of being on the move, but how time spent away nourishes the more mundane and static practices of family life. Holidays are earned through hard work, and the very act of going away is increasingly regarded as a necessary component of family life. What is intriguing about family holidays is how the ideal of this mobility is particularly celebrated by those publics that also lament the decline of the institution of the family *through* mobility. In the United Kingdom the popular tabloid press uses 'family holiday' promotions as a way of selling papers and subscribes to the ideal that the best way of celebrating family is not in situ in domestic space but through travel and breaking away from domestic routines.

Holidays are, of course, not always about getting away from the stresses and strains of family life but can also involve bringing families together. Celebrations like Thanksgiving and Christmas are meant to be all about family and giving everyone the opportunity to have time off at the same time so that the family can be together. At these times, family is reworked into a larger gathering of kin: having the 'family' around at Christmas suggests a wider grouping than the family that you might live with. However, as popular culture often reveals, these kinds of family gatherings are often far from straightforward. The temporary expansion of 'family' to accommodate a wider kinship group means having to negotiate more complex interrelationships; more often than not these are influenced by *a priori* moral judgements, and family members often anticipate how others will react in certain situations.

Family visits are also increasingly transnational. Mason's study of the family visit to Pakistan by people living in north-west England illustrates how these visits are for more than just visiting the family but are bound up with developing participants' sense of belonging in Pakistan. What is valued by the visit is the chance to get to know relatives in Pakistan, spend time together and to be there at key moments. Yet these visits also bring tension:

> For everyone, 'getting on' with relatives in Pakistan would inevitably sometimes involve dealing with, and challenging, prior assumptions and misunderstandings amongst both visitors and visited about cultural difference and similarity.
>
> (Mason, 2004b: 428)

Visiting family is therefore more than just reconfirming kinship ties but reflects on the self-identities of all those involved in the visit. While social and family lives require physical proximity (Boden and and Molotch, 1994), the realisation of the proximity is not always straightforward. Bringing the family together is not neutral, and what happens when family members get together is conditional on moral identities within family as well as differences and commonalities.

Non-linear mobilities, propinquity and conviviality

Mason's account of the visit is more than a discussion of the ephemeral quality of radial mobility that we might briefly experience in a two-week summer holiday; rather, it opens out both the social and spatial dimensions of family mobility. Discussions of family mobility should not be wholly inward looking, as this assumes a rather limited interpretation of family and falls short of the more diverse and active reading of family practices. By this I mean that both the causes and outcomes of family mobility are not just restricted to immediate family members but intersect with collective practices of community and neighbourhood. Thus an exploration of families on the move should not just be restricted to relations within families, but ought to be extended to other social groupings. This can be considered under the rather loose heading of non-linear mobilities: non-linear in that the focus is not on trying to join together dyadic relations, or map out individual mobility trajectories or even residential moves, but it is focused on the more varied, incidental and multidirectional mobilities through which proximity to others is experienced.

Before I consider the family practices associated with non-linear forms, it is germane to map out how the wider relationship between community and family is broadly understood and what the particular relevance of mobility is. Yet here there is no definitive account, as there is considerable variation in both populist and academic readings of community, family and mobility. The former tends to be dominated by the assumptions that mobility undermines family-based community and that both family and community have to be maintained despite mobility. The observation that family members no longer live close to each other or have time for each other is cited as a causal factor of decline of both trust and 'family values'. In contrast, academic scholarship has engaged critically with the dynamics of mobility and community, though in conflicting ways (see, for example, Savage et al., 2005). From one perspective, the haste and frequency of contemporary mobility is assumed to undermine social connectivities and social capital (Putnam, 2000). According to Bauman, we 'live in ruthless times... when people around seem to keep their cards close to their chests and few people seem in any hurry to help us' (2001: 3). In contrast, from a mobilities perspective, increased movement allows for more diverse and intense forms of connectivity (see, for example, Conradson and Latham, 2005; Larsen et al., 2006; Urry, 2002). There is also another distinctive theorisation of the association between mobility and community that emphasises a progressive sense of space (Massey, 1993). This locates the significance of community and neighbourhood in the process of boundary formation, which is magnified through mobility at different scales, from the local to the global (May, 1996).

What these different theoretical and ideological interpretations do share is a limited engagement with family. Few would therefore disagree with Edwards' assertion:

> The recent unhooking of family from blood and law, and of community from locality, however, has problematised the relationship between the two – family may be tangential to what is considered 'community' in contemporary individualised and globalised society.
>
> (2008: 5)

If family is no longer embedded in community, this is not to suggest that its uncoupling from place undermines the geography of family, but rather that the emphasis on locality has been replaced with a focus on networks (see, for example, Ryan, 2009, though the idea of the family network has been paramount since Bott's pioneering work in the 1950s: Bott, 1957). Family remains a forum for meeting up and an important reason for mobility. Moreover, because it is assumed that we are all living further away from family, considerably more work has to be put into making and forming these connections, because:

> average distances between members of social, familial and work-related networks have substantially increased since the 1950s; on average, social networks are more spread out and less coherent with fewer overlapping multiple affiliations.
>
> (Cass et al., 2005)

Yet networks do fall short of encapsulating the significance and vitality of non-linear mobility for a number of reasons. First, networks foreground individual points of connection; they are, as Bissell (2012) describes, conforming to a vision of mobility that is pointillist. Family networks, for example, draw together specific relationships: mother–daughter, aunt–niece and grandparent–grandchild. Networks based on family connections assume relations that are either known or can be named; hence relationships bring networks into being. There is a calculation inherent in pointillist mobilities suggested by the need to coordinate and synchronise meetings. In contrast, Bissell suggests that rather than proximity being a requirement of mobility, 'mobility itself generates multiple forms of proximity' (ibid.: 23). Proximity is not therefore defined as either the absence or the cause of mobility, and as such it is not given or fixed. Proximity and neighbourliness emerge out of the relations with others that we encounter through movement. Bissell's reworking of a more mobile sense of proximity is set against the tendency to map networks based on known relations with family, friends and colleagues that remain focused on individual end points of these mappings. Networks identify specific points rather than all points of connectivity, and prioritise those that make sense or are known to us because of their relational basis – such as ones based on family, friendship and work. This displacement of known others with unknown subjects, whom Bissell refers to as 'neardwellers', foregrounds the diversity of 'emergent relations' with others, which may or may not include family. In practice we do not maintain discrete 'networks' with family, neighbours and colleagues and so on, but rather the active and contingent nature of how these relations are maintained results in a more complex mesh of affinities.

Another limitation with networks is that the emphasis is on connectivity rather than doings. Networks foreground connections rather than practices. Families come together to celebrate, to eat together, to care for each other, to console, and to debate and argue. Yet the ways in which this happens are very fluid and dynamic; the boundaries of 'family' are as porous and loosely defined as any social grouping. Who comes together does not depend on a fixed set of relations but on the conditionality of family obligations (Finch, 1989). Judgements about who to invite and whether to attend family events are dictated not necessarily by biological and kinship relations but by the moral identities that are produced through these relations.

There is another issue to consider, which relates to the need to create grand narratives of social change. Cass et al. (2005), in their summary of networks, define what has happened to 'the average' network, but this is not a meaningful concept. Some connections may depend on very close points of contact, others are further away and the average might be somewhere in between but not relate to any actual distance travelled. It is also problematic to infer universal and unidirectional social change. For some people, living close to family remains an essential part of getting by, for others family practices can be maintained over distance (Mason, 1999), while some may resist the intrusion of family into their social worlds.

The problem is trying to make sweeping statements that bring together family, community and mobility, when reality is far murkier and unclear. As David Morgan (2008) suggests, the history of community studies is also one of the scholarship of boundary and identity and of community being as much about diversity and division as it is about homogeneity and reciprocity. This interpretation was recognised by scholars at the very inception of community studies back in the 1960s. Frankenburg, for example, suggested a very loose definition of community: 'a lot of people co-operating and disputing within the limits of an established system of relations and cultures' (cited in Morgan, 2008: 34). Frankenburg's definition is apposite today, but clearly resists being tied to any notion of social change; how can this reading of community be strengthened or diminished? However, it is also important to recognise the ease with which broad generalisations are made about the direction of travel that community and family life is heading in and that these observations are actually very rarely challenged. How often do you hear a commentator describe how 'the problem is that we don't live close to family anymore'? It is therefore very difficult to move on from the desire to write grand narratives of social change, which depend on being able to distil the 'average' or 'universal' character of something that is by its very nature diverse and fluid. These grand narratives depend more on ideology than empirical evidence and the need to explain social change, even if in practice the nature of this change is not linear but cyclical (Crow, 2008).

One way of trying to make sense of this opacity is to retell the accepted narrative of the uncoupling of family and community and to consider what lessons can be learnt from this narrative. I suggest that there is at best an inconsistency between theoretical and empirical accounts. Theoretically, family has been taken out of interpretations of community and neighbourhood, but empirically this is harder to sustain. The community studies of the 1950s and 1960s that first sought to unsettle the bond between community and family and move this research on to a more sociological and less geographical footing (Pahl, 2008) are no longer in vogue, though community revisits have been carried out in recent years (Charles et al., 2008; Savage, 2008). Yet even if it was possible to study community in its totality this would not assist in distilling a clearer narrative. A more reasonable project is to understand diversity and complexity rather than to make sweeping statements about causality.

Family and propinquity change

A reasonable starting point for trying to make sense of this complexity is the classic account of family as community, which it is assumed we have lost. Family as community through propinquity is most famously described in Young and Willmott's (1957) account of community in the East End. Their depiction of the resilience of a community based on working-class kinship that was produced and maintained principally through matrifocal ties resonates with ideological notions of family and community. Yet Young and Willmott's aim in their study was to identify the threats to this kind of community. They found that working-class kin-based communities had proved resilient to the extension of the welfare state, confounding assumptions that the state could and would replace support provided within families. Rather, the main challenge to kin-based communities was the decline of propinquity; as Young and Willmott's survey data demonstrate, the process of moving away from Bethnal Green reduced the frequency of kin visits. In the Bethnal Green study the high frequency of kin-based interactions depended on a very low level of mobility. One respondent famously reported not remembering another family other than his own move into his street for over 70 years. Hence the significance of kinship ties was not just their distribution across space but also the permanence of these ties. Kinship ties formed the basis of solidarity and community support, and as such the link between family and community is manifest and seemingly ineradicable. This finding that geographical proximity leads to greater frequency of contact between family members appears not only to be self-evident but to also have been repeated in more recent quantitative studies. For example, Mulder and van der Meer's (2009) analysis of a Dutch kinship study demonstrates that mothers, sons and siblings were more likely to give support to family members whom they lived closest to, and for all family members, living close to each other increased the likelihood of providing support.

Young and Willmott's analysis foregrounds the narrative of community decline through mobility. The assumption that mobility is the antithesis of community has considerable appeal. It is frequently assumed in public discourses and is rarely contested: mobility creates disjointed communities of newcomers and those left behind – no one belongs anywhere anymore. Families are assumed to be scattered over these fragmented communities as individual members move apart, thus destabilising family life. This depiction of the decline of social cohesion through mobility is well rehearsed in a number of commentaries on social change and the decline of community and social capital. For example, Putnam's 'social capital lost' thesis (Edwards, 2004, 2008) is based on a particular reading of the relationship between mobility on the one hand and proximity and social capital on the other.

The social decapitalisation thesis diverges from the community decline through mobility narrative in one important way. Putnam

(2000) accedes that in the case of North America, it is not distance that is the problem, but it is the speeding up and intensity of mobility that has brought about the fragility of social ties. Americans have not become more mobile in the latter half of the twentieth century with respect to residential change; in fact census data show that both long-distance and short-distance mobility have declined in recent years in the United States. Similar findings also hold for the United Kingdom. Shelton and Grundy's (2000) analysis of propinquity, as measured by travelling time between adult children and parents, comparing 1986 and 1995, illustrates that while the percentage of adult children living under half an hour's drive away from adult parents had declined over the nine-year period, the majority of adult children aged 18–54 had not moved far away. Data on frequency of contacts illustrate similar trends. McGlone et al.'s (1999) longitudinal analysis of British Social Attitudes survey data (comparing 1989 with 1995 data) on women's kin contact confirms a trend towards fewer weekly kin contacts for all categories of close kin (mother, father, adult child and sibling) as well as fewer contacts with close friends. In 1985, 59 per cent, 66 per cent and 65 per cent of women reported weekly meetings with mothers, adult children and close friends respectively; and in 1995 these percentages had fallen to 49 per cent, 59 per cent and 59 per cent, respectively. Thus the decline in contact between women and their close friends was less than that between mothers and adult children. This data from the 1990s for the United Kingdom can be interpreted in two ways: yes, there is evidence of a decline in kinship and friendship interactions, but the majority of women do maintain these relationships.

Recent revisits to community studies from the 1960s have also revealed more resistance to the assumed decline in family propinquity. For example, Charles et al.'s (2008) revisit of a 1960s community study in Swansea shows that while there has been an increase in geographical mobility, and as such the members of extended family kinship networks live further away from each other than they did in the 1960s, this trend is less significant for women and also for partnered respondents. Further analysis of the data does, though, reveal more subtle changes in relation to class. In the 1960s, working-class kin contact was closely associated with an uxorilocal pattern of kin contact (echoing Young and Willmott's identification of women as kin keepers). The reanalysis in 2002, while confirming the close association between working-class women and their kin, also found an important change in the pattern of men's kin contacts, with a noticeable decline in middle-class men's contact with their own families. In the study of 1960, 39 per cent of middle-class men had seen their mothers and 37 per cent their fathers in the previous 24 hours; at the time of the revisit in 2003 this has fallen to 16 per cent seeing their mothers and 29 per cent their fathers in the same time frame.

The question to ask, though, is what does the resilience of propinquity mean, given that it is not uniform? The findings from Swansea are not particularly surprising, and were evident in studies of geographical mobility in the 1960s that outlined the association between geographical and social mobility (Bell, 1968; Pahl and Pahl, 1971). What is intriguing about the Swansea findings is that this mobility remains a closed circuit and has not become more uniform over time, as might be popularly assumed. Clearly, therefore, any momentum towards dispersal is not uniform but is shaped by social identities; in Swansea this is revealed with reference to gender and class, but we may also assume that other identities, particularly ethnicity, are important (Savage, 2008).

The assumption of decline in propinquity, however, is so often voiced that it is too straightforward to dismiss with statistics on the resilience of living close to family. Hence for Putnam the 'problem' is not distance but the feedback loop between mobility and isolation. The damage to conviviality through churn is developed in accounts of disadvantaged communities. Anne Power's (2007) detailed study of community development in troubled city neighbourhoods starts from the premise that 'communities need families as the basic building block of social relations' and claims that:

> It is well documented that social relations were less transient, family relations more stable and community bonds stronger, even a generation or two age when families were larger and poorer, when modern amenities were not readily available and when work conditions were harder.
>
> (ibid.: 46)

What is at issue here in Power's communities is the problem of population churn, that is, many residents in disadvantaged communities are continually on the move. Thus it is not distance that is the problem, but that being on the move does not allow for a suspension of the competing desires to stay and go, which are necessary for the neighbourhood solidarities:

> Residential mobility is negatively correlated with social capital at the neighbourhood level. In communities with a high level of turnover, people tend not to get to know their neighbours or to put down roots. The pattern is self-reinforcing so tends to be stable over time.
>
> (Donovan et al., 2002: 24)

There are at least two contradictory readings of mobility: a progressive one whereby mobility and encounters with others reaffirm place, and a negative one in which no one knows each other anymore and it is the decline of 'knowing' that is destabilising. Despite Donovan's claim of churn being stable over time, it does not follow that community is bifurcated through mobility in this way, but rather that the interplay between community is more cyclical. Community is reinvigorated through mobility and can also become stagnant through immobility. These patterns do not necessarily become 'fixed'. Graham Crow (2008), for example, suggests that any demise and/or change in family and community life has been exaggerated. In particular, Crow suggests, drawing on Liz Stanley's discussion of social change (1992), that cyclical patterns are mistaken for linear transformations. This suggests a more nuanced observation of the relationship between mobility, family and community. It does not, therefore, make sense to try to condense either a linear model of distance or of social change, but rather to think about the diversity of the spatial geometry of family practices.

Tangled webs and informal care: The case for conviviality

One important dimension of the cyclical pattern of the spatial forms of family is that the practical need for physical proximity varies through the life course and is shaped by social identities. Who our neardwellers are is not neutral; as the data on proximity illustrate, working-class women are more likely to live close to family and others they have known 'all their lives'. In other words, neardwellers are more figurative and are not opposed to networks with known/named others. Who we encounter in proximity will be determined by age, gender, ethnicity or class, and so on. The contribution of feminist accounts of care is apposite to an understanding of this relationship between identity, community and propinquity. For example, Schaefer et al.'s (cited in Oakley, 1992) distinction between emotional, informational and instrumental support considers how distance limits how far people can engage in 'instrumental functions', namely 'the kinds of daily tasks involved in caring for someone such as transport, household assistance, meal preparation and shopping' (Ackers and Stalford, 2004: 136). However, it is not just gender that is implied in the relationship between care and distance. Wenger suggests that as people age, accessing a 'support network' becomes more relevant than sustaining strictly 'social networks' (1997). 'Support' does take different forms, though, providing a mixture of emotional support, companionship, instrumental help and information on a more or less daily basis. In practice, the character of the support network is likely to depend upon the relative significance of local neighbours, local family members and friends living within a few miles who are still mobile, and locally provide formal and informal services (Mulder and van der Weer, 2009).

Life course processes clearly shape the kinds of support and social networks that sustain families, not just at older ages, but when care for young children is needed. Childcare is one form of family practice and support that may be assumed to depend on spatial proximity; for young children, 'being there' means physical co-presence, and the expectations of parenting and childhood reinforce the importance of adult co-presence for children well into middle childhood (Reid Boyd, 2002). Thus, paradoxically, one of the 'trends' that may be assumed to undermine family and community, that is, mothers going out to work, is also implicated in the redrawing of networks of support around couples with young children. Wheelock and Jones' (2002) analysis of informal and formal childcare within the United Kingdom demonstrates that working mothers rely on both forms of support, as working mothers who make use of nursery or childminders will also ask family and friends to help out. Yet the most relied-upon source of support comes from maternal grandmothers, with around 70 per cent of employed mothers asking their own mums to help out. Just under half ask their fathers-in-law or their mothers-in-law to look after their children. Caring for children is, for most families, facilitated by locally embedded support networks,

and the old saying 'it takes a village to raise a child' is still pertinent for many families for whom the 'busy' nature of everyday life
enhances the need for help from immediate family members rather
than diminishing it.

Thus the kinds of support that families create and sustain over
time and place are not only complex, but differentiated, with some
families becoming more 'embedded' than others. In other words, to
recall Bissell, the kinds of relations that are experienced with 'neardwellers' are highly varied: for some, these encounters may be shaped
by functional need, while for others they can be more transient and
selective or even avoided. At the more functional end of the scale,
the kinds of affinities suggested by Jarvis' (1999) depiction of 'tangled webs' involve a whole cast of actors and agents, more than just
the conjugal couple and children, and embrace other activities than
are often acknowledged by the hegemonic focus on employment
and, to a lesser extent, childcare. Tangled webs of everyday family
practices do not just incorporate daily commuting, childcare and the
school run but also include leisure activities and consumption practices, including after-school clubs and visits to see and care for other
family members (for example, older relatives) as well as health-related
mobility such as trips to see doctors and dentists.

A final twist in the tale of the discussion about families on the move
is that, as Jarvis suggests, the more intense and embedded these non-
linear mobilities become and the more reliant they are on a complex
array of characters, the 'less' geographically mobile the individual
actors may become. According to Jarvis, 'it is rootedness within
socially and spatially systems of support which directly influence
household mobility strategies' (Jarvis, 1999). Jarvis (ibid.) suggests
that household mobility decisions should not be understood in
purely economic terms, as these depend as much on the non-material
social fabric that supports each household. She argues that to understand family's propensity to move, it is too simplistic to consider
only employment structures and opportunities, but, echoing Hanson
and Pratt (1988), we need also to consider the local embeddedness
of family, especially in terms of local support networks and family members' involvement in informal/formal economy. These kinds
of connections form a tangled web of interdependencies and subjectivities as notions of responsibility to others are interwoven into
individuals' attachments to place. Yet this degree of embeddedness

varies according to household structure. Households that can commodify support, for example by using formal childcare, have less need to develop informal networks, and the opposite causality can also be true in that families that are unable to develop these kinds of synergies are more likely to seek commodified solutions and therefore match their employment patterns to support this. Dual-career families are therefore less dependent on informal support and more able to access commodified care. In contrast, couples where only one partner works have less need to rely on informal support for childcare, but are more likely to draw on an informal economy for other sorts of help. In between these two types are the households that Jarvis describes as flexible, that is, those where there is a complex interplay between employment, care and support. These households often include one full-time and one part-time employee, and this employment arrangement is not sustained by formal childcare but by a dense network of informal support.

While a populist reading is that this intensification of work/life balance has undermined forms of connectivity, this causality does not hold up to close inspection; in fact the demands of combining work and family life may generate more complex networks, some of which need to be maintained over short distances. Locally situated support networks are disincentives to move as working parents come to rely on these sources of support in order to reconcile work and family life (Kan, 2007). Thus it is those who are *not* embedded in localised networks that move. Jarvis's observation of the inconsistency of modern capitalism is worth reiterating. She argues that the kind of work/family profile that is emerging as the most appropriate in late capitalism, which is where both adult family members are engaged in some form of employment, actually results in a geographically inflexible workforce. Reconciling work and family commitments is dependent on complex locally embedded networks of support that take time to create and may be difficult to dissolve. Moreover, the inflexibility of local networks can be further exacerbated through home ownership, as the costs of *individual* home ownership are often cited as a reason for the intensification of working time within families (Jarvis, 2005).

There is, though, one problem with this interpretation of differential forms of inter-connectivity, in that there is an underlying normative reading that less connectivity is more, at least in the sense that it does not restrict individual linear mobility. In contrast to Bauman's depiction of 'ruthless times', the intensification of the pursuit of individual consumption and a work/life balance can bring about more diverse forms of care and reliance on others, which may include other family members, neighbours or kin. This does not necessarily have to be reduced to the ideal of 'getting by', but can be expressed through a desire for conviviality. Realising that it is easier to get by through connectivity is an important line of resistance to the pressure to fulfil the neoliberal goal of individualised consumption that has also brought about 'disaffection with feelings of isolation and harriedness in a work-centred culture' (Jarvis, 2011: 561). Resistance to the intensification of modern life can be realised through seeking out other forms of connectivity that are less about getting by but more about slowing down the pace of life. Social networks may often provide both support and ways of reconnecting with places and other people. In recent years the promoting of community activities such as the 'Big Lunch' or shared national celebrations (even a royal wedding!) point to the enduring appeal of connectivity for its own sake rather than necessarily been channelled solely through the active embodiment of care or support. While we are not yet able to create what Ivan Illich in 1973 coined a 'convivial' society, which would guarantee all members equal access to community resources with the only limit being another member's equal freedom and access to resources. For Illich (1973: 11), conviviality is opposed to industrial productivity and encapsulates 'individual freedom realized in personal interdependence'. The desire and need for conviviality rather than isolation remain vital forces against the intensification of individual experience. As Jarvis (2011) remarks, proximity and social contact are not sufficient to engender forms of co-operation and support. Rather, these very much depend on active engagement, the mobilisation of community members and the synchronisation of activities, planned or otherwise, with others. Conviviality is also political, however, and individuals have many valid reasons for eschewing connectivity as well as reaching out to others. Thrift sees cities as 'oceans of hurt resulting from the undertow of the small battles of everyday life, but also as reservoirs of hope resulting from a generalized desire for a better future' (2005: 147). This generalisation brings together a diversity of desires and needs that depends on more than interaction; but also recognises the magnitude of this diversity. Street parties to celebrate royal weddings or jubilees will not necessarily be inclusive, but can reinforce social distance.

There is no universal story of long-term change in non-linear forms of family mobility and its interplay with other social forms, such as community. Grand narratives might be articulated, but these are more ideological than empirical. For some, a networked life maintaining connectivity regardless of distance is how social relations are managed and experienced. For others, reliance and need generate more complex forms of connectivity. Empirical research suggests that the opportunity for more spatially diverse and specific networks, as opposed to more embedded non-linear forms, is related to social identities, particular gender and class, and we can reasonably assume ethnicity as well. The unequal burden of care within family creates very different spatial relations, though these are not stable over time, but rather cyclical in nature.

Conclusion

This chapter has explored three rather more diverse themes of family mobility. In moving mobilities on from more economic forms, one difficulty is that the certainty afforded by the primacy of economic rationality is lost. Making sense of the complexity of mobilities while still retaining a sense of relationality between mobile actors is conceptually challenging. Moreover, these less tangible and predictable forms of mobility resist conforming to the grand narratives of social change that may help us to make sense of families on the move. There appears to be a widening gulf between ideological statements about family and mobility and subjective experiences. Rather than producing social change, the mobilities considered here sustain family practices while also decentring family life. Yet this decentring of family does not equate with decline. While the rise of spatially diverse and discrete networks is realised by some actors, it is not a uniform trend. For those most able to commodify the kinds of services and support that family and community might provide, a networked life is viable, but for others the very need to work, look after children and/or care for elderly or ill relatives is experienced through smaller scale non-linear mobilities.

This foregrounding of non-linear and nomadic mobilities suggests an incessant form of movement that does not allow mobility to stop. However, many mobilities are undertaken with the aim of reaching a destination, which may be spiritual, imagined and practical. The penultimate chapter of this book therefore considers the possibility of mobilities coming to an end.

6
Intimate Spaces

Any account of family mobility needs to consider when this mobility stops or is suspended. I do not mean by this to infer that there is a distinction between fixity and flow, but rather, echoing Harvey (1990), that places are fixed by relative permanencies and a truce emerges between the opposing sentiments and tendencies to move or remain fixed. Being intimate necessitates being close to others, both physically and emotionally, and being with other people, or by oneself, may be brought about by a suspension of mobility. This desire to cease mobilities, however temporary, or to dwell on it can be taken as a condition of human existence (Urry, 2002). Though as Bissell (2012: 5) discusses, drawing on Heidegger's discussion of dwelling, 'dwelling is an active process of accomplishment rather than a given'. One interpretation of mobilities is that it is through movement that spaces for intimacy, belonging and togetherness are created. In other words, we need to take into account the consequences and outcomes of mobility and the meanings of 'meeting up' and spending time together. But this suspension of mobility can only be temporary, as when physical mobility comes to a halt it is framed by the desire or need to move on or return. The very act of stopping mobility brings about the potential for other mobilities, which may be corporeal, imaginary or by proxy, such as through technology or material objects. As well as being emancipatory, these ongoing mobilities may be routine and repetitive, taking place within a house or some similarly limited space. We can think of the mobilities of housework or care that are implied by the suspension of mobilities that cross the boundaries of these limited spaces. Yet even if this truce is fleeting, a suspension of mobility can engender a sense of familiarity with a place or other people, and this feeling of familiarity can be reinforced by routine and repetitive movement. The overall theme of this chapter is the impossibility of mobilities coming to an eventual end; yet this also needs to be balanced out by recognising how mobility can be denied. For some, immobility is experienced as a trap rather than as part of the ongoing project of movement.

In this chapter, the relationship between mobility and intimacy is considered with reference to points of arrival and departure which might be about managing intimacy in a more limited and defined space or over distance. I begin this account by considering the relationship between home and intimacy. A key idea to develop this account is how home is in constant production though both corporeal and imaginary mobilities. This exploration of the dynamics of intimacy can be extended through cases of intimacies that are maintained both within and between different home spaces. This account of intimacy and home, though, does not just refer to individual subjectivities, but also to how these are shaped by gendered discourse and the differential mappings of male and female subjectivities with reference to home and mobility. I develop this account of the spatial dynamics of relationships with reference to the experiences of LAT couples and transnational families to extend the idea that intimate mobilities can never really 'stop'. Yet it is also germane to consider how intimate spaces may become ones that trap and imprison individuals in violent or oppressive relationships, and that for some it is not the impossibility of ceasing mobility that is at issue, but rather the impossibility of exit. In the final section of this chapter I consider how and when intimate spaces may be experienced as places of oppression.

Home

Departure and return

The concept of the dialectical home produced through mobility is well rehearsed, but, as I consider below, does not completely capture the dynamics of the production of home spaces. Numerous writers have described how movement is intrinsic to home as it is through travelling away from and returning home that its full meaning is appreciated. A sense of home or belonging is dependent on the spatial dialectic of home and movement. For example, Tuan (1974: 4) places the distinction between home and journey at the centre of his understanding of topophilia, or 'the affective bond between people and place or setting'. This active bond is realised not only in how individuals shape their own environments but also in how space and place shape subjectivity; to live one has to take risks in alien places. Porteous (1976: 390) identifies this distinction as one between home and non-home, or a 'fundamental divide between the small area of controllable space and the outer world of less-controllable space'; Sopher (1979: 134) suggests that the dialectic is realised as being that 'people want to make homes and people want to leave home'; and Relph (1976: 42) recognises that our experience of place, and especially of home, is a dialectical one, 'balancing a need to stay with a desire to escape'. Moreover, this dialectical understanding of home has considerable popular appeal. Possibly one of the most celebrated examples is Dorothy in *The Wizard of Oz*, who learnt through her travels in Oz that there is 'no place like home': only by leaving her home in Kansas did she come to appreciate what home, and her family there, meant to her. This interpretation of *The Wizard of Oz* is not novel, but rather epitomises a North American conceptualisation of home that emphasises rootedness and a sense of belonging. The tension between belonging and being on the road is a particularly important motif in American popular culture. It is not surprising to find that many contributions to scholarship on home and its meaning reflect this North American focus on the assumed tension between mobility and belonging.

Home, though, cannot be reduced to an account of individual transgression of the boundary between home and non-home without reference to how home is produced as a shared space. Unpacking what home means does not just reveal the significance of individual experiences but also how these experiences are shaped by shared meanings. Expectations about what home means are often manifested through ideologies of family and home. Home creates a place of sanctity and refuge, not just for the individual, but for family relationships. In our research with young people and parents in Britain, Spain and Norway, one of the most compelling findings was that when asked what home meant (notwithstanding the difficulty of translating the English word home into Spanish: see Holdsworth and

Morgan, 2005), both parents and young people alike in all three countries had a strong sense of 'security' and stability. However, this was also relational, in that for some respondents the security of home was associated with locking out the outside world and being on one's own, while for others it was about intimacy with family. In almost all of the interviews, questions about what home means elicited similar responses, such as:

> [s]omewhere I can just relax and be on my own if I want to be on my own. Somewhere I can feel safe ... But then, I suppose I always say, 'I'm going home.'

> What home means to me? ... I feel safe here. Um, I feel like I can do what I want here. And loved. I feel loved here. Yeah. It's just where you feel comfortable, isn't it? I feel comfortable, yeah.

> Wherever you've been, whatever's happened to you, you can come into your home, and you're safe, and you're with everybody who knows you.

Home is popularly celebrated as a place of refuge where we retreat from the outside world, and there appears to be a universality in this understanding of home. This essentialist interpretation is often associated with writing about the childhood home. For example, Gustave Bachelard (1964: 4) identifies the childhood home as 'our corner of the world' and describes the magical 'cosmos' of the childhood home and its imaginary spaces. Bachelard explores the potential of both mundane domestic arrangements and particular spaces within the home, primarily attic and cellar spaces, to provide refuge and stimulate imaginations. Bachelard's writings celebrate the emotional force of the childhood home and the perpetuation of this memory into adulthood.

Yet while writers such as Bachelard stress the essentialist qualities of home, historical research has sought to locate the development of home in particular social, economic and cultural contexts (see, for example, Rybczynski, 1986). The historian John Gillis argues that the relationship between city life and home were inverted and intensified as urbanisation developed during the nineteenth century and the middle classes retreated to the suburbs. Gillis suggests that middle-class Victorians withdrew into their homes and devoted both money and emotional work to the creation of home as a sanctuary in response to what Gillis summarises as 'their newly found malady of agoraphobia' (1996: 121). According to Gillis, home as haven and as a place to retreat from the outside world can be related to the emerging distinctions between public and private spheres. This does not necessarily mean that this boundary is secure and that the distinction between home and public space is as stark as the Victorian ideal would suggest.

The identification of home with security and stability masks other important qualities of home. The overall emphasis on the positive emotional force of home ignores the potential for home to be experienced as a dystopic space and one which, according to Mary Douglas (1991), children cannot wait to escape from, away from the tyranny of their parents. Sibley's (1995b) account of home experiences, based on mass observation archive data, also calls into question this essentially affirmative interpretation of home, and argues that home can be a prison and a locus of power relations just as much as a place of warmth and sanctity. Sibley (1995a) also acknowledges that scholarship on home has often struggled to see beyond its assumed cultural significance, and up until the mid-1990s little was written about its dystopic potential. I shall return to the dystopic qualities of intimacy, home and mobility later on in this chapter.

Thus, despite the initial appeal of the dialectical approach to home, we can also identify its limitations. In particular, it is not just that it reaffirms symbolic interpretations, but that the emphasis remains on distinguishing home from non-home, and the sense of movement between the two is lost. More recent contributions to the literature on space and mobility also query the significance of the dialectic reading of home. Urry (2007: 257), for example, suggests that 'if household members are regularly on the move then the distinction of home and away loses its analytical power'. One of the dangers of the dialectic interpretation is that it assumes balance between comings and goings, and these are clearly demarcated; in other words, it prioritises flow rather than constant flux. Dorothy, for example, only made *one* journey out of Kansas, yet for many people their comings and goings to and from home are more dynamic and less remarkable.

Rather than attempting to locate home in this boundary between public and private, it is more germane to consider if it is ever possible to draw a boundary between home and non-home or delineate home from anti-home or non-home? It is, as Massey (1992) rightly remarks, one of the paradoxes of home that it is not a fixed space – that home is always open and constructed by movement, and this suggests a different tempo and spatiality than that inferred from a strictly dialectic perspective. The point to consider here is that the active construction of home does not just occur through the movement between home and other places, but that home itself is always in construction, be it through our own activity or in our imaginations. This idea is developed by Fortier (2001, 2003) in her account of home and belonging among lesbian and gay young people. Fortier resists the notion that for these young people home is a place that has to be left behind. Instead, she contends that 'coming out' of the childhood home does not have to imply that childhood homes are too dystopic to be returned to; but that in treating home as a destination, rather than a point of departure, it is possible to consider how the home spaces that people move towards are related to those that are left behind. In her analysis of narratives of homecoming, Fortier (2001: 415) explores how these texts 'tell stories of *movement between homes*, ruminate on the relationship between geographical location and life's events, thus giving "place" a special significance as a result of its association with events in their life course'.

Yet Fortier argues that this does not mean that home, and specifically the family home, is rendered meaningless. Rather, she suggests that for these young people home is always in construction, and can be a place to revisit in the imagination, if not in reality. The significance of the imaginary is also developed in Elspeth Probyn's account of the impossibility of returning home; or at least if one does then it is only to realise that the childhood home is at best a cliché (1996). Probyn argues against an account of childhood as origin, but supports it as being one of the 'suspended beginnings' or 'beginnings that are constantly wiped out, forcing me to begin again and again' (Probyn, 1996: 101, quoted in Fortier, 2001: 412). For example, one narrative that Fortier discusses is Bob Cant's account of the 'two-mindedness' of lesbians and gay men and his reflections on his childhood home:

> It was only when I had been in London for some years as an openly gay man that I was able to re-examine my childhood and youth in a farming community in the East of Scotland. On some level I had behaved for years as if the gay man I became in London was

a totally new invention with no past. It took some time before I could acknowledge the enforced isolation of my youth and the impact which it had upon my whole personal development. Eventually I was able to look at the culture of normality which affirmed that 'everyone' lived in families and 'everyone' subscribed to values of the Church of Scotland. It was a culture which made me feel like an outsider; it was only after I left that area that I realized I was not the only outsider.

(Cant, 1997: 7, quoted in Fortier, 2001: 414)

In this extract Cant does not engage with a linear or procedural interpretation of home, but instead recognises that home is continually reproduced and reassessed. If not physically then at least emotionally, Cant is able to return home and start again and reassess not only his own but also others' identification with home. The significance of movement for home, therefore, is not just about corporeal mobility. Returning home and homecomings are structures of feeling that can be experienced through reimaging and reassessing earlier encounters as well as anticipating future events. The limitations of the logical extension of a dialectical interpretation of home are that from a dialectical perspective the emphasis is on home as distinctive from other spaces and the visibility of home/non-home boundaries. The problem here is that it reifies home as a place of stability and security. My suggestion is that the significance of movement, both imaginary and corporeal, to and from home does not necessarily consolidate boundary formation processes, but can emphasise home as a malleable space and how it is revisited and recreated in different ways over the life course.

Gender and life course

One important dimension of how the revisiting of home over the life course is differentiated relates to home as a gendered space. Fortier's theorisation of home through queer theory does more than consider the experiences of gay men and lesbians; it challenges the heteronormative interpretations of home. Feminist scholars have also used differential experiences of home to challenge normative assumptions about home and the gendered distinction between public and private space (see, for example, Bowlby et al., 1997; McDowell, 1983; Madigan et al., 1990). The differential mobility patterns of men and women to and from home frame and shape meanings of home, though the extent to which women's experiences of home are constrained by limited opportunities outside home is contested. On the one hand, women's mobility has opened up since the early Victorian era, and the kind of gender segregation described in Alderley Edge in the previous discussion of commuting (see Chapter 4) would be less recognisable today. The symbolic coupling of gender, particularly motherhood, with home is more lasting, though, and has not necessarily been displaced by women's changing employment activity. As Bev Skeggs (2004: 52) argues, while male subjectivity implies mobility, 'female subjectivity is mapped as a fixed place on the itinerary of the male journey' (cited in Bell and Hollows, 2007: 31). The boundary problem remains pertinent to gendered experiences of home. Even though women's lives are less constrained than their Victorian counterparts' by being at home, the cultural potency of domesticity and the expectations that women, particularly mothers, should 'be there' continue to shape the boundary between home and work. The emotional and cultural ties to home that persist and are reproduced through discourses of motherhood continue to tie women to an obligation to home that is distinctive from men's experiences (and also some women who are, according to McDowell (2006), becoming more like men). Moreover, as Gillis (1996) discusses, men do not necessarily experience any incompatibility between movements to and from home, and their return home is often celebrated by family practices: the normality of their being away is reaffirmed by the exuberance of returning home.

'Being there' does, though, engender complex emotions; it is too simplistic to assume that women are automatically oppressed within the home while men can enjoy a sense of privacy and sanctity, and this has been an important focus for research on gender and home. For example Saunders' (1990) empirical analysis of married couples' experiences of home in three English town in the 1980s did not reveal gendered differences, as both women and men expressed a positive emotional connection to home. His interpretation of these findings was that feminist interpretations of home were inaccurate and false. Yet his data do not necessarily substantiate this conclusion; in particular, Saunders has been criticised for his empirical methods as he interviewed couples together and thus failed to take a biographical perspective of individuals' experiences of home. Gurney's (1997) account of home draws on feminist epistemology to explore the emotional meanings of home and to challenge the divide between the economic and the emotional. Gurney was writing in the late 1990s, at a time, particularly in the United Kingdom, when the shift towards the economic values of home was emerging as a cultural trend, as house prices were increasing at a rapid rate and the possibility of making money from housing was becoming more popular and accessible. He resisted a materialist interpretation of home, arguing instead that the home was predominately an emotional space and that men and women presented very different accounts of meanings of home. Gurney's challenge to an economic and extensively 'rational' interpretation of home is now well established, and there is an extensive literature on emotional meanings and attachment to home (see Mallet, 2004 for a review of home literature). Yet Gurney's nascent attempt to capture the emotional quality of home remains valuable in that he explores the importance of biography in framing emotional attachment to home. Through the use of 'episodic ethnography', Gurney's account seeks to reveal how biographical events are defining moments in shaping individual orientations to home:

> [b]ereavement, falling in love, marriage and child birth have been crucial ways in which people have attempted to explain what home means to them. Home was defined *in relation* to these turning points.
>
> (1997: 383)

However, these events do not necessarily have the same impact on men and women. In particular, Gurney describes how childbirth can transform the home for women: in one case study, a mother's post-partum depression and experiences of isolation in the home left her feeling trapped and hating the place. Our emotional attachment to home is, therefore, often framed by the permeability of its boundaries and the extent to which we are able to maintain them. However, boundary work is a personal task and not one for which there is a cultural blueprint, in contrast to the symbolic qualities that are ascribed to home. Women's experiences of home, particularly in relation to motherhood, are not universal, for example while for some women motherhood might be associated with being isolated at home, for others it provides an opportunity to develop and sustain social networks (Head, 2005). Home space is not, therefore, a neutral space; it is certainly not a blank canvas onto which individuals can impress their own beliefs and emotions. Rather, these processes are constructed by social–cultural practices and ideas about how space, intimacy and family relations come together.

Displaying mobilities

One way of reconsidering the boundary issue of home is to consider how home is an expressive space for displaying mobilities. So the spaces that we acknowledge for privacy and emotional maintenance within a limited space can also be used to express affinities with other places as well as our mobile lives. Literature on domestic culture has considered the interplay between meanings of home, material culture and consumption (see, for example, Hurdley, 2006). With regard to mobility, the significance has almost exclusively focussed on the experiences of transnational families. Dowling and Blunt suggest that among diasporic communities home can be considered as a site for memory:

> In many ways, transnational homes are sites of memory and can be understood as performative spaces within which both personal and inherited connections to other remembered or imagined homes are embodied, enacted and reworked.
>
> (2006: 212)

Blunt and Dowling consider how the objects that are used to decorate the home, the style of architecture and other home-making practices materialise transnational connections. Home can, therefore be a place where culture and tradition are reworked and different landscapes are brought together, thus reflecting the permeability of home boundaries.

This also opens up an alternative perspective on gender and home, as these home-making practices of display are mostly done by women. Many diasporic women have a paradoxical relationship to home; it is a place of both containment and invisibility, but it is also a place of resistance. Home is both a space of adherence and subjugation to patriarchal relations. I shall return to consider this later on in this chapter.

Displays of mobility within the home are not only transnational. Mobilities may be displayed in the form of family holiday photographs or souvenirs. For these kinds of artefacts, the personal connection with the place where they originate from might be quite fleeting, but this does not necessarily infer that the memory they invoke is insignificant. Yet these displays can be interpreted as expressions of the self or a desire, maybe, to represent family and individuals as 'well travelled' and to recognise that family practices are not just restricted to the domestic sphere. Quite often, displays of mobility are mixed up with those that symbolise locality. In my home I have pictures and objects that were purchased when travelling abroad displayed alongside pottery from my 'home' town of Stoke-on-Trent, and when it comes to pottery I am usefully very careful to buy 'local' ware. Thus the expression of the self that I am seeking to reveal in these static displays is a dynamic one of both mobility and stability. Displays of holiday mementos will also incorporate an aesthetic quality, which may also reveal class identities. Displays of indigenous art from 'faraway' and 'exotic' places are a materialistic expression that family members have the resources to make these journeys. Other displays are clearly at the kitsch end of taste, either deliberately or not: collections of snow globes or fridge magnets, for example, can be ironic as well as used as a way to display the mobile self. Yet the assumption of corporeal mobility may also be a myth, because many objects will have been bought as presents by family or friends. When I travel with my daughter, she will always buy a fridge magnet for her father that will be displayed in his home, not ours.

Bell and Hollows (2007) make a similar argument for domestic culinary culture, in mapping out how traditional and authentic food cultures are identified with immobility in a globalised world. However, food can also be a way of celebrating and expressing mobility: cooking food first tasted on holiday is a celebrated display of mobility. The tension between the fixed and mobile cannot, though, be reduced to individual mobilities, but is bound up with the relationship between gender identities, mobility and domesticity. Bell and Hollows (2007: 36) conclude that 'the articulation of feminine and ethnic otherness, and their simultaneous fixing in a localized place in contemporary representations of culinary authenticity, helps to maintain mobility for some at the expense of immobility for others'. So the kinds of mobilities and relationships that can be expressed in these displays are very varied, and reveal the permeability of domestic boundaries and how these are bound up with the reproduction of social identities.

Home spaces and disclosing intimacy

Unpicking essentialist assumptions about home as a closed private space discloses the importance of mobility and movement and the permeability of home boundaries, and in doing so reveals inequalities in these processes. But the importance of movement and boundaries is not only realised as the divide between public and private space; it is also pertinent to consider experiences within the home and the importance of repetitive and routine mobility within the home. These mobilities might be of little physical consequence, yet they are bound up with the dynamics of relationship and power within the home.

Again, the middle-class Victorian home offers an intriguing glimpse of how power dynamics are made manifest through spatial segregation in the home. Following Goffman (1959), different rooms within the home can be interpreted as the loci for front-stage and backstage activities. Moreover, this distinction between these functions often literally follows the historical spatial ordering of rooms. The front, or best, room was for receiving guests and formal occasions, and could be contrasted with the backstage settings in the kitchen and nursery (see Gillis, 1996). In this way, both gender and age distinctions were reinforced through boundary regulations within the home. Victorian attitudes to the spatial organisation of childcare are particularly revealing. The middle- and upper-class ideal was of the segregated nursery, where children slept, ate, played and studied under the guidance of a nanny or nursemaid. Interaction with adult members of the household was maintained through limited, episodic encounters. The Victorian nursery not only served to reinforce spatial distinctions between children and other family members, but its design also attended to children's mental and physical well-being (Holdsworth, 2012). Adequate ventilation was required to ensure children's health, while toys, colour schemes and furniture were designed to maximise children's mental stimulation. In addition, the nursery not only segregated children from their parents, but from their peers. Social and spatial segregation during childhood were mutually reinforcing. Children from working-class neighbourhoods did not enjoy the same material comforts as their middle-class peers, but their greater 'freedom' was also associated with greater risk, particularly because of the environmental health hazards endemic in Victorian slums, where diarrhoea and respiratory disease were the main killers of infants and young children (Woods, 1996). Both in- and out-of-home spaces contributed to poor health, through insanitary overcrowding indoors and environmental hazards outside. The working-class home offered little sanctuary from these perils.

The Victorian ideal of segregated childhood is certainly not one that would be extolled by contemporary childcare experts, but that does not mean to say that boundary issues are of less importance within contemporary homes. Rather, more fluid and dynamic experiences of home which are associated with a more democratic distribution of resources and space are still shaped by spatial–temporal rules that govern behaviour and relationships within the home. Wood and Beck's (1994) celebrated study of one room in Denis Wood's family house seeks to uncover the litany of rules through which a home is created from its material form. From this detailed ethnographic study they reveal how, for children, a home is a 'field of rules' (1994: 1) through which they are indoctrinated into the values that adults imbue into material artefacts. Rules to control children's movement (don't touch, don't run) reinforce adult views of the value of things. The home, however, is not a static space, but one which is continually unfolding. The rules incorporate adults' memories of their own childhood homes, and as such the room is an 'instantiation of a kind of collective memory' (Wood and Beck, 1994: xv).

Negotiation of spatial–temporal rules in the home is intimately bound up with moral identities and parent–child relationships (see, for example, Valentine, 1999). Sibley's (1995b) analysis of home lives, using data from accounts of middle-class childhoods in the United Kingdom Mass Observation Archive, explores the tension between parents' desire for order and children's lack of concern for regulation and orderliness. Sibley associates the home, and the boundary struggles that emerge from this tension, as a locus of power relations. Using a dichotomy of parenting styles derived from Bernstein's distinction between positional and personalising families, he identifies different ways in which these power relations and associated modes of control are deployed in the home (Sibley and Lowe, 1992). The positional parent relies on their authoritative position to dictate what happens and where, thus maintaining strict boundaries, while personalising parents will assume a more equal distribution of power, and so the use of space and time within the home becomes more flexible and negotiable.

Writings on children's negotiation do, though, as Sibley suggests, counterpoise adults' expectations about home against that of children's. An underlying assumption is that regulation and boundary control are necessary to mitigate conflict, but home is also a place for disclosing intimacy as well as regulating behaviour. In addition, boundaries are not just restricted to spatial and temporal controls: boundaries of intimacy are maintained (and transgressed) within the home. A shift towards emphasising intimacy rather than regulation is in part in recognition of a more democratic approach to family life. As discussed in Chapter 2, the emergence of democratic family practices and the resulting transformation of intimacy have been key components of individualisation, though also one aspect of family life that has been contested. Although I have considered the limitations of the democratic family at various times in this book, particularly with reference to gender and mobility, it would seem reasonable to assume that contemporary parenting is more likely to be based on democratic principles that espouse open dialogue rather than un-negotiated rules. It is too simplistic, though, to assume that home has shifted from being a location of control to one of disclosing intimacy. Rather, family practices within the home respond to both domains: regulations and rules are not just directed to reinforcing the material value of home spaces and artefacts, but also attend to the formation and experiences of family intimacy.

Disclosing intimacy within the home and the mechanisms through which personal intimacy between family members is valued (but also regulated) often depend on a 'dialogic' ethos that emphasises the need to talk and the importance of sharing experiences and emotions between family members. Yet how intimacy is disclosed is not just dependent on conversation, but is bound up in the appropriation of home space, particularly the need for privacy within the home. Jaqui Gabb's (2008) mapping of intimacy in families explores how privacy is a gift that family members grant to others. Using the example of the relationship between a mother (Harriet) and her teenage daughter (Kelly), Gabb compares how intimate space is experienced for both Harriet and Kelly. For Harriet, giving Kelly space in the home and allowing her to shut her door when her friends are visiting is predicated on retaining the 'right to intrude' (Ibid.: 101). Harriet maintains that this right is reciprocal: her door is always open to Kelly. Hence while Harriet's gift of privacy is based on the mutual respect for the other's need for privacy and openness, Gabb suggests that the mother in this case is able to maintain control over the daughter's 'right' to privacy:

> [t]he rhetoric of openness and principle of democracy are part of this family's practices, but only insofar as they can be fashioned to achieve parental preferences.
>
> (Ibid.: 101)

Negotiations of space within the home are about regulation and control of individual movement, and they are also central to how relationships within the home are developed and maintained. Moreover, these kinds of rules and more tacit understandings are always in construction. The regulation of space and distance, while still allowing for the disclosing of intimacy, has to be balanced to meet the needs of all family members. Conventionally it is often assumed that it is up to parents to give space and support to young people and that it is young people's emotions and indentities that need to be managed within the home. However, it is more appropriate to adopt an intergenerational perspective here, that is, that the needs of all family members have to be negotiated within shared family space and that parents are the beneficiaries as well as the givers of support and intimacy. All family members have a need for privacy within the home as well as for opportunities to get away from home. Echoing Gurney's description of feeling trapped within the home, the regulation of space and movements in and out of the home is meaningful to all family members. Thus the focus on children's needs and behaviour within the home may presuppose that parents have more fixed and achievable behaviours. In our study of leaving home (Holdsworth and Morgan, 2005), interviews with parents revealed not only how they had to negotiate their children's changing needs and behaviours within the home but how they could also feel frustrated by their own domestic lives. For example one mother in the Liverpool study discussed at length her obsession with tidiness and order, and related this to her relationship with her husband, who was an alcoholic and had very little engagement with home and family life; he just came and went and left everything to her:

> And I think if I had the house tidy and straight I'd feel better and I'd have more patience with the children. But that's – at the end of the day does it matter about the house? But I get, it gets, well, I think I get obsessed by it, I know I do. About trying to keep it tidy... You know, but I mean, I feel as if we are being just taken for a – for granted, like he's using this house to sleep in and sit and watch the telly, and drink, and that and, he's not contributing to it as a family and we are not a family any more.

Behaviours in the home were, in this case, interconnected. There was very little interaction between the husband and the rest of the family, which created its own tensions that the mother expressed through her anxieties about tidiness. Her commitment to the domestic space can be contrasted with that of her husband's, which was shaped by a distinctive mobility regime and limited interaction. Her anxiety was because she was unable to achieve the order she wanted both in her home and in her relationship with other family members. Other examples of the complexity of intergenerational intimacy include young adults in lone-parent families, particularly women, who recognised the need to support their parent (especially mothers), and as a consequence were reluctant to leave home if this meant leaving their mother on their own or without appropriate support (Holdsworth, 2007). One Norwegian daughter of a lone parent described the difficulty that her mother faced when she left home:

> No, actually, it has only been us two at all times then, so she is probably more dependent on me than I'm on her, or was, I think. I think it was worse for her that I left for myself than it was for me then.

These findings echo Diana Leonards' (1980) empirical study of intergenerational relations in working-class families in Swansea. Leonard describes how parents, particularly mothers, were anxious to 'keep' their children close by and did not actively seek to encourage young people's departure from the parental home. In these communities mobility was restricted, or at least very limited. While Leonard's account of controlled mobility can be interpreted as a form of community reliance, other experiences are more personal.

Space, privacy and mobility are all integral to disclosing intimacy. It is not just the comings and goings from home that are relevant, but the subtle and less remarkable interactions within home spaces that are interwoven into accounts of family and personal intimacy. Creating space to be together as well as to have time alone is a recurrent theme of family practices. Not all family members are treated equally when these practices are worked out, however, and expressions of intimacy are not always democratic. Conventionally we might recognise how children's movements are restricted within the home, and in turn how children may challenge these restrictions. Yet both inter- and intra-generational relations are often complex and paradoxical: giving freedom to children may be resisted by parents if it undermines opportunities for parental expressions of love and intimacy.

The value of a mobilities interpretation of home is that it moves beyond the dynamics of the dialectic between home and away from home to consider a more active construction of home over time that recognises the value of imaginary and remembered journeys and experiences, as well as ideals of home that look to the future rather than the past, and does not fall into the trap of assuming the ubiquitous quality of its symbolic meaning. Home is a warehouse of complex emotions, and this applies to homes currently inhabited as well as those remembered. However, the challenge in attempting to distil this dynamic interpretation of home is to maintain the focus on mobility and movement. One way of overcoming this is to consider families and intimate relationships which foreground mobility. In the following sections I turn to family practices and relationships that are experienced over distance by considering the experiences of LAT couples and transnational families.

Boundary work, relationships and intimacy: Living-apart-together couples

When thinking about the interplay between space and intimacy, Rossi's (1956) observation that it is easier to adapt to an excess of space, that to manage a lack of space, reveals how material space shapes and defines opportunities for intimacy and privacy within relationships. So for couples who can afford to do so, moving to a larger house is a way of managing the interconnection between space and intimacy, while for others maintaining separate households offers an alternative way of managing relationships. The experiences of this latter group, or LAT couples, provide an intriguing challenge to the primacy of physical co-presence in relationships. The choices and experiences of couples who retain separate residences will be very varied, though there has been a tendency in empirical studies to focus on the experiences of professional couples living within the same locality (Holmes, 2004). A note of caution here is that maintaining close relationships over distance is certainly not a new phenomenon, and couples have often had to live apart due to resource constraints and the need to take up employment or look for work elsewhere. Mass mobilisations of workers in the nineteenth century often resulted in LAT relationships, though these were assumed to be formed out of necessity, rather than choice. Levin (2004), who has carried out the most detailed research on LAT couples to date, suggests that contemporary LAT couples maybe be divided into two groups: those who would like to live together but cannot and those who choose to live apart. The former group includes couples whose responsibility for others precludes moving in together. This is often associated with the presence of children from other relationships, though it can also be associated with the need to provide care for another relative, such as an elderly parent, or those for whom work commitments (or study commitments) effectively mean that they have to maintain two separate households. The spatial dynamics of the two types of LAT relationships can be distinctive, with the former more likely (though not necessarily) to be maintained over distance, while the latter, as Roseneil (2006) describes (albeit in a small qualitative sample), are often involved in relationships within a locality. However, the limitations of Levin's dichotomy is that it assumes that couples have clearly stated reasons for their domestic arrangements, and that they are either willingly chosen or regretted due to conflicting circumstances. Roseneil (2006) suggests that a more common experience is that couples are not sure of why they live apart, but rather that these couples were in relationships that 'were not constructed within a framework in which living together was something about which to decide' (8.15).

Among couples for whom the need to maintain separate house-holds reflects other caring needs, in particular the presence of children from a previous relationship, protecting the physical space within which relationships with children are sustained is prioritised. Therefore, this form of LAT relationship does not necessarily under-score the importance of physical co-presence, but recognises the difficulty of sharing space between different kinds of relationships. There is, though, an important underlying spatial tension in these arrangements. On the one hand, space provides the opportunity for intimacy (particularly with children), but on the other it protects and defines independence and separation and limits the interaction between all those involved in the LAT relationship. Being physi-cally apart provides a solution for parents in particular to negotiate potentially competing demands from children and new partners. Likewise, in the absence of any logistic or caring need to maintain two separate households, the choice to retain two residences is often framed through the need to retain 'independence' within the rela-tionship. Thus both forms of LAT couples are potentially generating distinctive spatial and mobile dimensions of intimacy.

It is not surprising that one of the common themes that emerges from accounts of living arrangements and boundary negotiations for LAT couples is the emphasis on the need to retain control and privacy. This is a common reason given by LAT couples for not want-ing to live together: the fear of losing control over one's own space through letting someone else into this space. For couples who do not want to live together, this could be associated with painful mem-ories of separation, the need to protect children's inheritance or a general desire to maintain independence. Elderly women in LAT rela-tionships may continue to choose to maintain separate homes as a way of balancing intimacy and autonomy (Ghazanfareeon Karlsson and Borell, 2004). Women are also more likely to favour LAT rela-tionships than elderly men, as keeping their own home is a way of confronting male oppression that women may have experienced in previous relationships (Ibid.). This suggests a different interpretation of LAT couples and democratic intimacy, in that while it does afford more individual control it often emerges out of prior experience of undemocratic relationships. The ability to control one's own space is highly valued by women who have not been able to do so in the past. So while closeness is a prerequisite for intimacy and for caring

(Holmes, 2006), these caring practices are gendered, as it is women who are expected to provide most of the care. Thus the choice not to live together can be seen as offering women more opportunity for equity in relationships, in that they can negotiate their caring role by *not* being there. Normative assumptions about mobility and intimacy are effectively gendered, as women provide a caring role within geographical proximity and this is facilitated by their lack of investment in other spheres. LAT arrangements can facilitate a reconfiguration of caring practices and intimate relationships. The emergence of varied forms of intimacy in different spatial configurations appears to be in response to a reconfiguring of gender roles, rather than a radical challenge to and detraditionalisation of gendered expectations about caring (see Adkins, 2002).

LAT couples who choose to live apart in response to individual expectations of autonomy and independence defy convention about co-residence and coupledom, but at the same time recognise the importance of individual control over space and self-esteem. Is it loss of independence that is feared from moving into together? One of the interesting findings that emerges from research with LAT couples is the trade-off between shared intimacy and intimacy at a distance. For example Roseneil (2006) recounts the case of Philip, who recognised the benefits of living alone and the freedom that this entailed – particularly around food and the need to compromise (about what food is provided and when) – but at the same time was aware that he could develop a fuller sense of self through sharing and taking responsibility for others. This distinction reflects distinctive theorisations about the self and (in)dependence. Conventionally, emotional and economic independence are valued and stress the need for looking after number one. But as feminist writers such as Morwena Griffiths (1995) theorise, a distinctive understanding of the relationship between the self and others is one that recognises how a sense of self is enhanced through care and responsibility we have for others. Co-presence forces us to consider the needs of others over seemingly minor but essentially important issues, such as food and the regulation of everyday activities. The need to compromise and fit in with others' tastes and demands is an important part of building and maintaining relationships. In Philip's case, he acknowledges that compromise can enhance relationships and that compromise is essential in intimate relations, while enjoying the freedom of being able to do his own thing through living on his own. Paradoxically, though, the fact that these compromises are not made every day but are only negotiated when the couple is together highlights the significance of this negotiation, which is that a meal, for example, is cooked *for* someone else, rather than as part of the practices of everyday family life. By maintaining two physically distant residences, couples can reaffirm the choices and practices they make when they are together.

On one level, LAT relationships could be viewed as disinvesting in intimacy as a way of protecting oneself against the uncertainties of contemporary relationships and gendered practices. Alternatively, LATs can provide a way of protecting intimacy and only sharing the most intimate aspects of everyday life and leaving the more unremarkable ones, such as dealing with washing, cooking and cleaning, to individual decision-making. The assumptions of research on mobility and households have been that the household is the unique locus for intimate relations and that couples are dependent on sharing physical space to develop intimacy. Research on LAT relationships illustrates how permeable these assumptions about shared space can be and that intimacy might be supported by time spent apart. LAT couples also highlight the significance of flux rather than flow, as for many the ultimate goal is *not* to live together, which may be assumed if it is taken that LATs are the logical outcome of the difficulties of combining work and intimate relations. Research on these couples discloses the limitations of this assumption. For couples who either elect not to cohabit or for whom living together is not how they frame their relationships, the comings and goings between homes that create time apart and together may reaffirm intimacy, friendship and closeness.

Belonging and mobility: Transnational families

The experiences of LAT relationships reveal a complex interplay between mobility, intimacy, space and emotion, yet for these couples the geographical scale over which they are played out is, for the most part, quite defined, and relationships are sustained through movement between two clearly defined and controllable spaces. Nonetheless, families and intimate relationships are not restricted to defined geographical scales, but can and do extend over more varied and greater distances. The experiences of transnational families provide another perspective on the ways in which individuals maintain networks and sustain relationships over national boundaries and the impossibility of these transnational mobilities coming to an end. The maintenance of households across national boundaries is not a new practice (see, for example, Ballantyne and Burton, 2009; Skrbiş, 2008), though this practice is very dynamic, and the contemporary experiences of transnational families are not necessarily analogous to bi-national families in the past. Contemporary accounts of transnationalism foreground the ways in which 'individuals, groups and organisations are presumed to operate across national borders and are reliant upon ongoing commitments which straddle those borders' (Heath et al., 2011: 1.2). This emphasis has stimulated interest in the practices of everyday life among members of transnational families that acknowledges the significance of all family members regardless of their mobility status (see, for example, Bryceson and Vourela, 2002; Goulbourne et al., 2010). So rather than considering the experiences of those who leave and how they adapt to their mobility, it is more germane to develop a dynamic understanding of mobility that considers how people actively maintain ties to origins and destinations despite mobility.

The experiences of transnational migrants reveal the complex ways in which intimacy is maintained over distance and the importance of material exchanges as well as the use of technology. Thus, 'the economic and emotional aspects of relationships are virtually impossible to distinguish' (McKay, 2007: 191). Material exchanges will include financial remittances as well as goods and artefacts, and artefacts can be both symbolic and practical. In non-western contexts, being able to display western goods is aspirational and suggests upward mobility of the family group. Moreover, these exchanges are not necessarily intended for the immediate family only, but may be offered to a diverse kinship group. Both the sending and the receiving of material objects as well as travelling with diasporic material artefacts are not just about material exchanges, but can be analysed using the concept of extended personhood (McKay, 2007; Parkin, 1999). Senders are able to maintain their local identity through these material remittances. Objects of interest are not just those that are kept by an individual that are inscribed by their own memories of self and personhood, but include those that are sent. These financial transfers and goods have to be translated on the ground, though; money has to be spent or invested by kin and visibly witnessed in the receiving community, while artefacts have to be displayed by others within the kinship group. Thus the flow of money and goods in maintaining an absent presence is facilitated by agents – or avatars – who, either through investing money, displaying artefacts or using goods (for example, wearing clothes), simultaneously maintain migrants' visibility in the local community and negotiate their identity within the familial and communal group within which their extended personhood is located. The sending and receiving of artefacts can therefore be understood as the perpetuation of mobility and the maintenance of an absent presence in communities that are left behind. Even if corporeal mobility is temporarily halted, the sending and receiving of artefacts can maintain relationships across national boundaries.

Communication technology also speeds up these processes of exchange. Transnational migrants from the Philippines in McKay's (2007) ethnographic research received text messages requesting financial support for family members, so, creating an immediacy to material exchanges that heightens their expressive function. As Levitt writes, new technologies 'heighten the immediacy and frequency of migrants' contact with their sending communities and allow them to be actively involved in everyday life there in fundamentally different ways than in the past' (Levitt, 2001: 22). As such, the time–space compression of everyday lives facilitates and sustains transnational care and intimacy. Yet the experiences of transnational families in maintaining long-distance intimacy is by no means universal but is shaped by access to resources as well as gendered and radicalised practices (Parreñas, 2005). The experiences of mothers living away from children and their maintenance, from a distance, of their relationships with their families of origin through emotional labour can be quite different from childless transnational migrants or those with fewer dependents.

Key themes to consider here are those of belonging and rootedness and how these are sustained through memory, communication and economic transfers as well as visits. This raises a tension that is a recurring theme throughout this book, which is equating the opportunities afforded by mobility, which, in the case of transnational migrants, are usually concerned with either securing economic or human capital advantage, with the advantages of sustaining belonging and rootedness. Yet, as Svaşek (2008) describes, this does not mean that there is a neat relationship between stability and belonging on the one hand and mobility and longing/homesickness on the other. Rather, these should be conceptualised as emotional processes that highlight the constancy of emotional connection with certain places:

> 'Belonging' or 'feeling at home', in other words, should not be defined as a static form of rootedness in one physical locality, but can best be conceptualised as a cognitive and emotional process in which people identify with particular experiences and feel familiarity with their lifestyles.
>
> (Svaşek, 2008: 215)

Feelings of home and belonging, therefore, are not necessarily reduced to stability. Belonging as familiarity is in keeping with the overall theme of this chapter, which is that mobility can never fully stop. The relationship between familiarity and stasis varies, however, for individuals. Some people feel at home in extreme mobility and would find it difficult to get used to a more sedentary lifestyle, while for others geographical proximity to significant others is more important. Accounting for how individuals express either distance or local reasoning, however, is more problematic. Mason (1999) argues that the extent to which individuals can negotiate relationships over distance is incorporated into the moral identities that are formed through obligations to others. The 'good' child, for example, may be identified with adult children who remain in touch and visit parents, and other relatives, on a regular basis. Moving away may be facilitated by trust that relationships will be maintained over distance.

Cultural and social context are also important, however, and we should be wary of universalistic interpretations of both care and intimacy, (McKay, 2007). Transnational migrants have to negotiate expressions of care and emotion in distinct cultural contexts, and it is this ability to be able to perform care in different localities that sustains these transnational experiences. Moreover, the transitional experience also challenges the primacy of co-presence. Urry's (2002) account of co-presence highlights how it is worked into different obligations that we have for 'being there', which range from legal, familial and social, to time and place, yet these obligations are not necessarily equated with practical issues of care. Rather, for transnational migrants, the obligations of 'being there' are replaced, in the most part, by emotional and financial expressions of care that can be translated by others into material benefits or embodied acts of love and care. This is not to say that those who are absent are not missed, but rather that it is too simplistic to assume that intimacy is channelled primarily through co-presence. Accounts of transnational migrants challenge the assumption that intimacy implies physical co-presence. Hence, while it might be reasonable to assume that intimacy precludes mobility and geographical distance, in practice it can be sustained over different spatial configurations. Being able to have a presence that is not configured through face-to-face encounters is, as Drotbohm argues, 'highly valued as an explicit demonstration of transnational solidarity' (2009: 16).

Transnational intimacy does, though, require a different set of strategies to those of LAT couples within more closely defined localities, for the distance associated with the former is not about control and independence, but rather the challenge is to maintain attachment and intimacy over distance. Thus intimate spaces, in particular those where care is performed and given and received by others, are not closed spaces. Those who are absent can still be present in very practical ways, and the perpetuation of movement can be sustained through the transfer of material artefacts as an expression of care.

Trapped

If what I have argued above against a universalistic interpretation of intimacy is correct, then it would seem reasonable to conclude that intimacy is not only contextual but also that it need not be ubiquitous or benevolent. For example, descriptions of diasporic homes and displays of artefacts identify the home as a site of resistance as well as one for reconfirming multiple belongings and identities (Blunt, 2007). While one of the overarching assumptions of individualisation is that individuals are free to move on to form new relationships and new forms of intimacies that revolve around the self, it is germane to consider the validity of this supposition. In her critique of individualisation, Smart (2007) makes the valid point that not everyone is free in this way, and that the emphasis on choice effectively negates the lived experiences of those who are unable to move on for some reason. Being trapped in a relationship could be the result of threats from a violent partner; financial constraints (in the recession of 2009, the UK media discussed the plight of couples who were forced to live together in a house that they could not sell, even though they had formally separated or divorced); or because of cultural sanctions that make leaving a relationship difficult. Others may feel trapped in a relationship that they are not able to move on from for less tangible reasons that incorporate a range of emotions concerning the strength of belonging and the seeming impossibility of moving on and living somewhere new or changing one's life. Smart suggests that 'embeddedness and connectedness are therefore not to be taken as *a priori* good things' (2007: 137). If these forms of embedded connections are so controlling that they do not afford any opportunity for change (and the possibility of exercising individual choice) then they could be more limiting than enabling. The distribution of individual freedom is not, therefore, universal, but rather is shaped by social identities, particularly gender, class, race and sexuality.

Smart's argument about embedded connections echoes Sibley's criticism of scholarship on home discussed at the beginning of this chapter, which is that academic research has been biased towards utopian readings of intimate spaces. Sibley summarises the dominant approach in the literature as follows:

> I think it fair to say that most studies of behaviour in domestic environments in the last twenty years have depicted the home in benign terms. It is a refuge, a source of comfort in a world otherwise replete with tension and conflict, and the only environment in which individuals can function as autonomous agents.
>
> (1995a: 93)

Challenging this benign ideal of home and revealing its dystopic quality has been resisted on a number of fronts. Thus the struggle of both victims of domestic violence and feminist campaigners to have the legitimacy of the lived experience of women and children recognised was initiated by the disclosure of extreme forms of domestic violence by campaigning scholars in the 1980s such as Elisabeth Stanko (1985) and Dobash and Dobash (1992). Their research brought to public attention the intensity and frequency of domestic abuse. However, domestic violence remains a taboo and a misunderstood subject, both in academic writings and popular discourses.

But do these experiences have to be polarised? Can home be both nurturing and constraining? Even for victims who are forced to flee dangerous and violent homes, this does not necessarily diminish the powerful emotional force of home. In addition, many victims of domestic violence feel they are unable to leave. This could be due to their economic position and the cultural association of women's place in the home (Veness, 1992). For some women, the home is so restrictive that leaving home is a transgression of women's identity and role. Women who leave often have to face up to the shame of separation and the impact that this has on those involved, particularly children. Places of safety and refuge do offer a space for intimacy that individuals could not escape to on their own, yet this does not mean that these places offer a refuge in the way that is associated with domestic homes; they are refuges only as a place of last resort.

The sense of shame is a recurrent theme in accounts of domestic violence. The difficulty that women have in talking even to close friends and family about their experiences and the reluctance of others to challenge behaviour are recurrent themes in victims' accounts. This sense of isolation is often reinforced by physical separation; as Warrington (2001) reports, women victims of domestic violence were often cut off from their friends and family by their abusive partners, and this separation can reinforce a sense of social and spatial restriction. Victims' feelings of shame and their articulation of self-blame reveal their powerlessness. Smart remarks perceptively that in personal life, 'anxiety and powerlessness are intimately linked' (2007: 140). For victims of domestic violence, this statement would seem somewhat of an understatement, but it does offer an understanding of why women blame themselves for their own experiences.

Feelings of being trapped are not just restricted to physical constraints on the daily movements of victims of violence. Entrapment can arise due to mobility limitations; the disabled, the elderly and the infirm often find the physical difficulty of getting out prohibitive, and then the boundary of home becomes a physical barrier that is difficult to cross (Imrie, 2004). Thus while the home is symbolically celebrated as a place of sanctuary and security, these symbolic constructions reinforce the sense of anomie of those who are left 'housebound'. Not being able to get out not only restricts opportunities for meeting other people, but can also be injurious to mental and physical health. Embodied experiences of home change over the life course, so what was once a place of refuge can become a prison due to frailties and physical weakness. The ability to construct and transgress boundaries, therefore, is not fixed but changes over time.

The experience of being trapped, either by another person or by one's own limited corporeal mobility jars with more fluid constructions of home and intimate space discussed at the beginning of this chapter. This therefore opens the question of how permeable boundaries are maintained. Other arenas of social science consider how individuals respond to changing circumstances and declining fortunes. I suggest that Albert O. Hirschman's (1970) classic formulation of exit, voice and loyalty strategies in response to decline in organisational performance may be applicable to an account of intimate spaces. In Hirshman's model, the two main strategies of exit (leaving without trying to fix things) and voice (speaking up and trying to remedy the defects) are opposed; that is, if exit is favoured as a way of responding to organisational failure, this will dampen the effectiveness of voice. But the choice between exit and voice is socially and culturally contingent. Hisrchman (1970: 272), referring to a liberal reading of North American history, observes that the 'preference for the neatness of exit over the messiness and heartbreak of voice has then persisted throughout our national history'. In the North American model, upward mobility achieved through exit, that is, moving on and leaving those less fortunate behind, while seeking solidarity with others through voice has had less individual and political appeal. Choosing voice over exit only makes sense through the expression of loyalty, which can engender a desire to remain and sort things out, rather than taking the easier or expected option of moving on. This balance between exit and voice can be taken as the idealised way of experiencing home and intimate spaces, that is, being able to leave is the preferred way of managing these spaces. Accordingly, for those not able to use exit strategies, voice is also muted; it is those who have a choice between exit and voice and those who can choose to stay or go who are more effective in using either strategy. So the experience of being trapped is not just restricted to limited opportunities for exit and mobility; other ways of expressing identity and control are also muted. This recalls the discussion of home realised through departure and return at the beginning of this chapter. It is not only realised movement that defines intimate spaces but also the possibility of movement and the option of being able to leave that is central to being able to create space for dialogic intimacy.

Conclusion

If immobility is the outcome of mobility, this does not mean that mobility can come to an end, but rather that a truce between the desire to move on and the desire to stay is temporarily achieved. This truce consolidates and anticipates corporeal mobility, but also, imagined and remembered forms. It does, though, allow for a sense of familiarity which can be associated with belonging and a sense of home. Yet how this is arrived at and what it signifies is not universal, nor can it be reduced to individual subjectivities. In particular, the fixing of female subjectivities in place at home is bound up with women's experiences and also with their assumed immobility that allows for the mobility of others. Hence rather than identifying home as the outcome of movement, home can be experienced through both the mobility and fixidity of others, and this suggests a more dynamic relational interpretation of home. Yet the relational home does not depend on co-presence, for when mobility does lead to absence, maintaining presence can be achieved in more imaginative ways. And while home for most people is experienced through relational mobilities, its most dystopic form denies mobility. Hence, while home might be associated symbolically with security and locking out the outside world, this sense of withdrawal depends on the freedom to leave. If this is denied, the home is no longer defined by permeable boundaries and dialogical relationships, but rather by the impossibility of being able to return if these boundaries are breached.

7
Conclusion: Decentring Family and Intimate Mobilities

This account of family and intimate mobilities defies a neat conclusion, as the intention is to reveal the variability of movement that interweaves the collective and the individual. Sometimes this fusion is transparent, for example moving house or going on a family holiday. Yet the collective affinity of family mobilities is not just revealed when families move together but also in how individual mobilities sustain or reconfigure family practices. This fusion can be emancipatory and beneficial, though at other times it is restrictive or forced. Intimate mobilities also pertain to the control of relationships; again, this can be intended or intangible. Time together and time apart are interwoven into intimacy, and the compulsion to achieve proximity is mediated by the desire for privacy and separation. Mobilities also infer immobility, as they are defined by both points of departure and points of arrival and how these settings are created and maintained through movement. In summary, the dynamics of family mobility cannot just be tied to the present, but are formed in the past and anticipate the future:

> Who we are derives in part from the multiple connections we have to other people, events and things, whether these are geographically close or distant, located in the present or past. This constellation of others may influence us in diverse ways, acting via physical encounter and somatic internalisation, in response to the power of images and narratives, and through the operation of memory and desire.
>
> (Conradson and McKay, 2007: 167)

As the limits to mobility are extended both geographically and temporally, the very subject of family and intimate mobility becomes unclear. Conventionally, family mobility may be taken to refer to clearly demarcated practices such as moving house or leaving home, but, as I have argued, these events imply other (im)mobilities, and it is not always possible to delineate these movements from other practices. This suggests an account of family mobilities that is continually unfolding, though punctuated by temporary truces, but one in which movement in any direction or immobility bring about movement or stasis in a different form.

As a way of drawing this account to a conclusion, I consider two themes that are central to developing a research agenda on family and mobility. The first relates to the wider context of family mobility and how it is interpreted by different publics. The second theme relates to methods for the analysis of family and intimate mobilities and the challenges inherent in studying the family outside its structured and static form.

Public challenges

The project of decentring family through mobility can also be conceived as part of the task of rescuing family from its ideological constraints. Family mobility is subject to scrutiny, regulation and control, which can both re-centre or decentre family life. My intention has not been to write about what the family ought to be or what it could achieve, but how family is and how these practices are shaped by both past and anticipated events. Hence this account of family and intimate mobility has been set against grand narratives of how the force of mobility in late modernity has impacted on family life. The need for propinquity and immobility is situated against a portrayal of social breakdown through mobility. One story to write about family and intimate mobilities is that mobility undermines connections to family, friends, community and locality. This idea about family and mobility refers to a range of emotions and practices that appeal to our sense of belonging, neighbourliness and rootedness and locate our personal relationships within geographically bounded space. This assumption that family life is undermined by mobility is mostly concerned with longer term fixed mobility that recognises how people move away from each other (though never closer to others), but also incorporates a sense that our busy mobile lives are incompatible with family and community life. This supposed relationship between family mobility and community underscores contemporary political and popular discourse about declining communities and people's everyday contribution to where they live. The assumed process is straightforward: as individuals become more mobile and move away from their communities of origin, they lose touch with their family members and fail to re-create a sense of belonging in communities into which they move. This version of family mobility is one that is often told and retold, confirmed by media reports that lament the decline of 'family and community values'. 'Research' reporting how few people know or trust their neighbours (enough to leave a key with their neighbours, for example) is frequently reported and associated with the 'modern' practice of mobility. Consider the following headline from the *Daily Telegraph* in November 2008: 'Britons know just nine neighbours by name: Britain's neighbourhoods are in sharp decline, with people knowing just nine of their neighbours by name, according to a survey' (Butterworth, 2008).

The article refers to 'research' carried out by an insurance company about how safe people felt in their neighbourhood, and documents the decline in neighbourliness. The reason for this decline is easily identifiable by a spokesperson for Neighbourhood Watch, an organisation that directly promotes community support and 'neighbourliness', who comments that the problem is mobility, and that neighbourhoods have been undermined as families are so much more mobile now compared to how they used to be when families 'stayed in one house for a lifetime'. The spokesperson goes on to suggest:

> It is one of the good things that could come out of the credit crisis if people cannot afford to move and have to put down roots instead. People would get to know one another and all our findings show that this helps to improve safety levels.
>
> (Ibid.)

The desire for community through propinquity is therefore political, and conviviality can provide a form of resistance to the anonymity and displacement of life on the move. In this populist interpretation, mobility creates disjointed communities of newcomers and those left behind – no one belongs anywhere anymore. Families are assumed to be scattered over these fragmented communities as individual members move apart, thus destabilising family life. Mobility is imagined as a centrifugal force that drives us away from each other and one that undermines how we value both familial and informal connections with those we encounter in our everyday lives. People move around; they do not form sustained relationships with people to whom they live near, and they are not part of their local communities. Moreover, this reading of family mobility is positioned in relation to other 'economic' mobilities and how the former is constructed as inferior to the latter. Economic rationality assumes the pursuit of individual mobility. Laments about the dispersal of family are expressed simultaneously with concerns about how the lack of mobility is indicative of individuals' incapacity to better themselves. This primacy of exit as the rational strategy for self-preservation in the economic sphere is legitimated as it meets individual needs; the impact on collective affinities is collateral damage.

My response to this account of the relationship between mobility and family contests two fundamental assumptions that relate to the supposed tension between mobility and family practices and the patterns of mobility that are assumed to be in the direction of dispersal only. What is at issue here is the necessity of resisting the need to centre the family and fix it as an immobile group. Accounts of family practices, at different geographical scales, reconfirm the durability of practices that are not dependent on passive readings of the family:

> The realm of the 'family' continues to retain its significance in the face of distance, dispersal and translocality even as the desire to go on being a family under such conditions is occasionally ruptured and continually reworked.
>
> (Yeoh *et al.*, 2005: 308)

This active recognition of the realm of family does not, though, reduce it to individual agency; if family continues to have significance it is in how it takes shape and form through practices that are shared and experienced collectively. Yet this sense of collectivity is not necessarily benign. It is too easy to assume that a family setting is nurturing and inclusive, as against the unfeeling and alienating experience of other realms. The reworking and rupturing of family can be both forceful and restrictive; it can bring about mobilities that are unintended or not sought for, as well as limit the possibility of mobility. Victims of domestic violence and stalking have their own mobilities narratives that are set against individual freedom. Family practices may also negate individual reflective agency through being more bound up with the unthinking and habitual nature of practice. This is an important codicil to the mobilities paradigm that emphasises purposeful action and intention; for example, the concept of meetingness implies individual agency, purpose and freedom. Yet the durability of family is that it resists the need for a purpose for all journeys: many mobilities are simply 'done'. While the desire to do family may be transparent and articulated, the practices that sustain this are not always equally celebrated.

My second critique of the grand narrative is the universal assumption of dispersal. At different places in this book I have called into question the assumption that propinquity is in decline and that networks are necessarily maintained over greater distances. In transport studies, the possibility that developed economies are moving towards 'peak car', as evidenced by a reduction in both car sales and per-capita distance travelled, is interpreted as an outcome of demographic change as well as a cultural shift in attitudes to car ownership and independent mobility (Pearce, 2011). As the global population ages, a reduction in personal mobility might be anticipated, but this trend is not just apparent among older age-groups; younger people are delaying learning to drive and owning a car. Explanations of 'peak car' suggest the importance of technological developments that mitigate the need to travel, or more economical drivers, as the cost of personal mobility is increasing. Another undeniable global trend is the increase in population density. As the global population passes the seven billion mark, it is inconceivable that this will result in the hyper mobility of all individuals; there are some very mobile people, but for most, the reality of getting by is getting on with the people who we live in ever closer proximity to. These near dwellers are not distinct from family, friends and work colleagues, but are formed from these overlapping affinities. Yet who these near dwellers are is closely linked to identity, and there are important variations in age, class, gender, ethnicity and sexuality. Thus, while it is not possible to isolate family from other social forms, it is necessary to resist the need to have grand narratives, as these assume that we all start from the same point, move in the same direction and end in the same place.

Methodological challenges

This recognition of the variability of mobility raises significant methodological challenges. Law and Urry (2004) show how existing empirical methods deal poorly with the fleeting, multiple, non-causal, chaotic, complex and sensory nature of mobilities which are implied through considering material and social realties through movement. In their account of mobilities 'on the move', Büscher and Urry (2009) review the varied ways in which mobility can be captured, recorded and visualised. Their contention is that the theoretical challenge of mobility necessitates a re-vision of empirical inquiry.

Meeting the challenges of mobile empirical inquiry in the twenty-first century can draw upon the technologies that make so much of late-modern mobility possible. Mobility methods are expanding to capture the variability and randomness of mobility, for example mobile phone records, location-sharing apps, social media and visual mobile methods, including video and still cameras, all facilitate the recording of mobilities. Thus the various technologies that some observers suggest are leading to the decline of mobility can also be seen as facilitating how we see and experience the mobility of others. Studies that follow people can do so physically, by walking or travelling with others, or by shifting the locality of inquiry to places through which mobile subjects pass through (see for example Laurier et al., 2008; Weilenmann, 2003). Quantitative methods have also developed to extend the remit of mobilities research, though in a very different direction. The greater availability of longitudinal data and modelling strategies to analyse these data allow for migratory movements to be understood in relation to other events and social identities.

Despite these advances, there are issues yet to be resolved for empirical studies of mobility. For methods to be operationalized, they require a clearly defined start and end points. Social sciences methods, either qualitative or quantitative, focus on what can be observed rather than what cannot. The expansion of quantitative data on movement over time depends on the ability to record events and fix boundaries around units of data collection. Quantitative analysis therefore reveals patterns of long-term household mobility, but the data sets on which these analyses are based can reveal very little about patterns of propinquity. The permeability of household boundaries suggested by the linking of mobile and immobile family practices does not fit with the requirements of survey data collection that depend on being able to locate individuals within precise parameters, such as a household or an organisation. For qualitative methods, the emphasis on following a narrative can generate a complex record of what happens at the expense of what does not occur. In our research on leaving home, for example, those young people who had left home due to difficult circumstances and who were reliant on voluntary services to find housing were monosyllabic in their response and found it difficult to talk about their experiences. An emphasis on narrative or following people can make it tricky to record these kinds of difficult, unexpected or resisted events. Revealing the unintended or forced circumstances of mobility is less straightforward than more emancipatory and active accounts. Narratives can also be accounts of the self which do not necessarily foreground relationality. Techniques such as family ethnography can open up this aspect, though not always in straightforward ways. As researchers move beyond the privileged position of the individual narrative, shared accounts are conditional on the relationships between those involved. The politics of disclosure can also limit what it is possible to reveal to family members about observed relationships and intended or unacknowledged outcomes for others within the family. In some families involved in our research with parents and children, both generations sang from the same hymn sheet and mutually endorsed the similar accounts of individual mobility; in other situations, however, contradictions between individuals were as fascinating as the observations of shared understanding. Revealing these contradictions can, though, put a strain on the position of the researcher as confidante within the family.

Technological advances that facilitate the recording of mobilities can meet some of the challenges of developing family and intimate mobilities research. However, we need to be alert to the kinds of mobilities that are made easier to record by the use of these advanced technologies: those that are observed, acknowledged and delineated. The potential of family and intimate mobilities extends beyond these forms of movement to consider the intricacies of linked (im)mobility and the impacts that practices have on others, both individually and collectively. It is in realising the complexity of how movement brings people together and moves them apart, in celebrated and mundane ways that the potential of family and intimate mobilities can be realised.

The mobilities turn calls for a re-visioning of the social through mobility; in doing so it will not simply map the intricacies of individual mobilities, but will reveal their complexity. Mobilities bring about and sustain relationships of dependency as well as facilitating, or denying, independence. Yet how family practices can be reclaimed from ideology and structure through a mobilities paradigm brings its own sets of challenges. Family can be usefully understood as a constellation of mobilities, yet the challenge is to reveal the relationality between these and the ongoing tensions between flow and stasis.

Bibliography

Aassve, A., Billari, F. C., Mazzuco, S. and Ongaro, F. (2002) 'Leaving home: A comparative analysis of ECHP', *Journal of European Social Policy*, 12, 259–275.

Ackers, L. (2000) 'From "best interests" to participatory rights: Children's involvement in family migration decisions', *Child and Family Law Quarterly*, 12(2), 167–184.

Ackers, L. and Stalford, H. (2004) *A Community for Children?: Children, Citizenship and Internal Migration in the European Union* (Aldershot: Ashgate).

Adey, P. (2006) 'If mobility is everything then it is nothing: Towards a relational politics of (im)mobilities', *Mobilities*, 1(1), 75–94.

Adey, P. (2010) *Mobility* (London: Routledge).

Adkins, L. (2002) *Revisions: Gender and Sexuality in Late Modernity* (Maidenhead: Open University Press).

Ahmed, S. (2004) *The Cultural Politics of Emotion* (Edinburgh: Edinburgh University Press).

Ahmed, S., Castaneda, C., Fortier, A-M. and Sheller, M. (2003) *Uprootings/ Regroundings: Questions of Home and Migration* (Oxford: Berg).

Allan, G. and Phillipson, C. (2008) 'Community studies today: Urban perspectives', *International Journal of Social Research Methodology*, 11(2), 163–173.

Atkinson, W. (2011) 'From sociological fictions to social fictions: Some Bourdieusian reflections on the concepts of "institutional habitus" and "family habitus" ', *British Journal of Sociology of Education*, 32, 331–347.

Bachelard, G. (1964) *The Poetics of Space* (New York: The Orion Press).

Bailey, A. (2009) 'Population geography: Lifecourse matters', *Progress in Human Geography*, 33(3), 407–418.

Bailey, A., Blake, M. and Cooke, T. (2004) 'Migration, care, and the linked lives of dual-earner households', *Environment and Planning A*, 36, 1617–1632.

Ballantyne, T. and Burton, A. (eds) (2009) *Moving Subjects: Gender, Mobility and Intimacy in an Age of Global Empire* (Chicago: University of Illinois Press).

Barker, J. (2009) ' "Driven to distraction?": Children's experiences of car travel', *Mobilities*, 4(1), 59–76.

Barker, J. (2011) ' "Manic mums" and "distant dads"? Gendered geographies of care and the journey to school', *Health and Place*, 17, 413–421.

Barker, J., Kraftl, P., Horton, J. and Tucker, F. (2009) 'The road less travelled – new directions in children's and young people's mobility', *Mobilities*, 4(1), 1–10.

Bauman, Z. (2000) *Liquid Modernity* (Cambridge: Polity Press).

Bauman, Z. (2001) *The Individualised Society* (Cambridge: Polity Press).

BBC (2012) *Rambings*, Available at http://www.bbc.co.uk/programmes/b006xrr2, date accessed June 2012.

151

Beck, U. (1992) *Risk Society: Towards a New Modernity* (London: Sage).
Beck, U. and Beck-Gernsheim, E. (2002) *Individualisation: Institutionalised Individualism and its Social and Political Consequences* (London: Sage).
Becker, G. S. (1981) *A Treatise on the Family* (Cambridge: Harvard University Press).
Bell, C. (1968) *Middle Class Families: Social and Geographical Mobility* (London: Routledge and Kegan Paul).
Bell, D. (2006) 'Bodies, technologies, spaces: On "dogging" ', *Sexualities*, 9(4), 387–407.
Bell, D. and Hollows, J. (2007) 'Mobile homes', *Space and Culture*, 10, 22–39.
Berlin, I. (2002) *Liberty: Incorporating Four Essays on Liberty*, H. Hardy (ed.) (Oxford: Oxford University Press).
Bernardes, J. (1998) *Family Studies: An Introduction* (London: Routledge).
Bissell, D. (2012) 'Pointless mobilities: Rethinking proximity through the loops of neighbourhood', *Mobilities*, forthcoming.
Blunt, A. (2007) 'Cultural geographies of migration: Mobility, transnationality and diaspora', *Progress in Human Geography*, 31, 684–694.
Boden, D. and Molotch, H. (1994) 'The compulsion of proximity' in R. Friedland and D. Boden (eds) *Nowhere: Space, Time and Modernity* (Berkeley: University of California Press), pp. 257–286.
Bonnet, C., Gobillon, L. and Laferrère, A. (2010) 'The effect of widowhood on housing and location choices', *Journal of Housing Economics*, 19, 94–108.
Bott, E. (1957) *Family and Social Networks* (London: Tavistock).
Bourdieu, P. (1992) *A Theory of Practice* (Oxford: Polity Press).
Bourdieu, P. (1996) 'On the family as a realized category', *Theory, Culture and Society*, 12(3), 19–26.
Bourdieu, P. (1998) *Practical Reason: On the Theory of Action* (Stanford: Stanford University Press).
Bowlby, S., Gregory, S. and McKie, L. (1997) ' "Doing home": patriarchy, caring and space', *Women's Studies International Forum*, 20, 343–350.
Boyle, P., Cooke, T. J., Halfacree, K. and Smith, D. A. (2001) 'Cross-national comparison of the impact of family migration on women's employment status', *Demography*, 38(2), 201–213.
Boyle, P., Cooke, T. J., Halfacree, K. and Smith, D. (2003) 'The effect of long-distance family migration and motherhood on partnered women's labour-market activity rates in Great Britain and the USA', *Environment and Planning A*, 35, 2097–2114.
Boyle, P., Kulu, H., Cooke, T., Gayle, V. and Mulder, C. H. (2008) 'Moving and union dissolution', *Demography*, 45(1), 209–222.
Bryceson, D. and Vuorela, U. (2002) 'Transnational families in the twenty-first century' in D. Bryceson and U. Vuorela (eds) *The Transnational Family: New Europe, Frontiers and Global Networks* (Oxford and New York: Berg), pp. 1–30.
Büscher, M. and Urry, J. (2009) 'Mobile methods and the empirical', *European Journal of Social Theory*, 12(1), 99–116.
Bushin, N. (2009) 'Researching family migration decision-making: A children-in-families approach', *Population, Space and Place*, 15(5), 429–443.

Butcher, M. (2011) 'Cultures of commuting: the mobile negotiation of space and subjectivity on Delhi's metro', *Mobilities*, 6(2), 237–254.

Butterworth, M. (2008) 'Britons know just nine neighbours by name', *Daily Telegraph*, 25 November. Available at http://www.telegraph.co.uk/news/uknews/law-and-order/3521251/Britons-know-just-nine-neighbours-by-name.html, date accessed January 2012.

Cass, N., Shove, E. and Urry, J. (2005) 'Social mobility exclusion and access', *Sociological Review*, 53(3), 539–555.

Castells, M. (1996) *The Rise of the Network Society* (Malden and Oxford: Blackwell).

Charles, N., Aull Davies, C. and Harris, C. (2008) *Families in Transition: Social Change, Family Formation and Kin Relationships* (Bristol: Policy Press).

Christie, H. (2007) 'Higher education and spatial (im)mobility: Non-traditional students and living at home', *Environment and Planning A*, 39, 2445–2463.

Clark, W. A. V. and Davies Withers, S. (2009) 'Fertility, mobility and labour-force participation: A study of synchronicity', *Population, Space and Place*, 15, 305–321.

Clark, W. A. V. and Huang, Y.Q. (2006) 'Balancing move and work: Women's labour market exits and entries after family migration', *Population, Space and Place*, 12, 31–44.

Conradson, D. and Latham, A. (2005) 'Friendship, networks and transnationality in a world city: Antipodean transmigrants in London', *Journal of Ethnic and Migration Studies*, 31(2), 287–305.

Conradson, D. and McKay, D. (2007) 'Translocal subjectivities: Mobility, connection and emotion', *Mobilities*, 2(2), 167–174.

Cooke, T., Boyle, P., Couch, K. and Feijten, P. (2009) 'A longitudinal analysis of family migration and the gender gap in earnings in the United States and Great Britain', *Demography*, 46(1), 147–167.

Cooke, T. J. (2008) 'Migration in a family way', *Population, Space and Place*, 14, 255–265.

Courgeau, D. (1985) 'Interaction between spatial mobility, family and career life cycle: A French survey', *European Sociological Revue*, 1(2), 139–162.

Cresswell, T. (2006) *On the Move: The Politics of Mobility in the Modern West* (London: Routledge).

Cresswell, T. and Merriman, P. (2010) *Mobilities: Practices, Spaces, Subjects* (Aldershot: Ashgate).

Crow, G. (2008) 'Thinking about families and communities over time' in R. Edwards (ed.) *Researching Families and Communities: Social and Generational Change* (London: Routledge), pp. 11–24.

Cull, M., Platzer, H. and Balloch, S. (2006) *Out on My Own: Understanding the Experiences and Needs of Homeless Lesbian, Gay, Bisexual and Transgender Youth* (Brighton: Health and Social Policy Research Centre).

Détang-Dessendre, C. and Molho, I. (1999) 'Migration and changing employment status: A hazard function analysis', *Journal of Regional Science*, 39(1), 103–123.

Dobash, R. and Dobash, R. (1992) *Women, Violence and Social Change* (London: Routledge).

Donovan, N., Pilch, T. and Rubenstein, T. (2002) *Geographical Mobility* (London: Performance and Innovation Unit).

Douglas, M. (1991) 'The idea of home: A kind of space', *Social Research*, 58, 287–307.

Dowling, R. and Blunt, A. (2006) *Home* (London: Routledge).

Drotbohm, H. (2009) 'Horizons of long-distance intimacies: Reciprocity, contribution and disjuncture in Cape Verde', *History of the Family*, 14(2), 132–149.

Edensor, T. (2007) 'Mundane mobilities, performances and spaces of tourism', *Social and Cultural Geography*, 8(2), 199–215.

Edensor, T. (2008) 'Mobility, rhythm and commuting' in T. Cresswell and P. Merriman (eds) *Mobilities: Practices, Spaces, Subjects* (Aldershot: Ashgate), pp. 189–204.

Edwards, R. (2004) 'Present and absent in troubling ways: Families and social capital debates', *The Sociological Review*, 52(1), 1–21.

Edwards, R. (ed.) (2008) *Researching Families and Communities* (London: Routledge).

Elliott, A. and Urry, J. (2010) *Mobile Lives* (London: Routledge).

Felstead, A. and Jewson, N. (2000) *In Work, At Home: Towards an Understanding of Homeworking* (London: Routledge).

Ferguson, H. (2009) 'Driven to care: The car, automobility and social work', *Mobilities*, 4(2), 275–293.

Finch, J. (1989) *Family Obligations and Social Change* (London: Polity Press).

Finch, J. (2007) 'Displaying family', *Sociology*, 41, 65–81.

Flowerdew, R. and Al-Hamad, A. (2004) 'The relationship between marriage, divorce and migration in a British dataset', *Journal of Ethnic and Migration Studies*, 30, 339–351.

Fortier, A. -M. (2001) ' "Coming home": Queer migrations and multiple evocations of home', *European Journal of Cultural Studies*, 4(4), 405–424.

Fortier, A. -M. (2003) 'Making home: Queer migrations and motions of attachment' in S. Ahmed, C. Casteñeda, A-M. Fortier and M. Sheller (eds) *Uprootings/Regroundings: Questions of Home and Migration* (Oxford: Berg), pp. 115–136.

Frändberg, L. (2009) 'How normal is travelling abroad? Differences in transnational mobility between groups of young Swedes', *Environment and Planning A*, 41(3), 649–667.

Franklin, A. and Crang, M. (2001) 'The trouble with tourism and travel theory', *Tourist Studies*, 1(1), 5–22.

Furlong, A. and Cartmel, F. (2007) *Young People and Social Change: New Perspectives* (Maidenhead: OUP).

Gabb, J. (2008) *Researching Intimacy in Families* (Basingstoke: Palgrave Macmillan).

Ghazanfareeon Karlsson, S. and Borell, K. (2005) 'A home of their own: Women's boundary work in LAT-relationships', *Journal of Aging Studies*, 19, 73–84.

Giddens, A. (1992) *The Transformation of Intimacy: Sexuality, Love and Eroticism in Modern Societies* (Cambridge: Polity Press).

Gilding, M. (2010) 'Reflexivity over and above convention: The new orthodoxy in the sociology of personal life, formerly sociology of the family', *The British Journal of Sociology*, 61(4), 757–777.

Gillies, V. (2011) 'From function to competence: Engaging with the new politics of family', *Sociological Research Online*, 16(4), 11. Available at http://www.socresonline.org.uk/16/4/11.html 10.5153/sro.2393.

Gillis, J. (1996) *A World of Their Own Making* (Oxford: OUP).

Goffman, E. (1959) *The Presentation of Self in Everyday Life* (New York: Doubleday Anchor).

Goldberg, P. J. P. (2011) 'Space and gender in the later medieval English house', *Viator*, 42(2), 205–232.

Goody, J. (1996) 'Comparing family systems in Europe and Asia: Are there different sets of rules?', *Population and Development Review*, 22, 1–20.

Goulbourne, H., Reynolds, T., Solomos, J. and Zontini, E. (2010) *Transnational Families: Ethnicities, Identities and Social Capital* (London: Routledge).

Granovetter, M. (1973) 'The strength of weak ties', *American Journal of Sociology*, 78, 1360–1380.

Green, A. E. (1997) 'A question of compromise? Case study evidence on the location and mobility strategies of dual career households', *Regional Studies*, 31(7), 641–657.

Green, E. A. and Canny, A. (2003) *Geographical Mobility, Family Impacts* (Cambridge: Joseph Rowntree Foundation, Policy Press).

Griffiths, M. (1995) *Feminism and the Self: The Web of Identity* (London: Routledge).

Grosz, E. (ed.) (1999) *Becomings: Explorations in Time, Memory and Futures* (Ithaca: Cornell University Press).

Gurney, G. M. (1997) ' " ... Half of me was satisfied": making sense of home through episodic ethnographies', *Women's Studies International Forum*, 20, 373–386.

Gustafson, P. (2009) 'More cosmopolitan, no less local', *European Societies*, 11(1), 25–47.

Hägerstrand, T. (1970) 'What about people in regional science?', *Papers of the Regional Science Association*, 24, 1–12.

Hajnal, J. (1965) 'European marriage patterns in perspective' in D. V. Glass and D. E. C. Eversley (eds) *Population in History* (London: Arnold), pp. 101–143.

Halfacree, K. (2004) 'Untying migration completely: De-gendering or radical transformation?', *Journal of Ethnic and Migration Studies*, 30(2), 397–413.

Halfacree, K. and Boyle, P. (1993) 'The challenge facing migration research: The case for a biographical approach', *Progress in Human Geography*, 17, 333–358.

Hanson, S. and Pratt, G. (1988) 'Reconceptualizing the links between home and work in urban geography', *Economic Geography*, 64(4), 299–321.

Harvey, D. (1990) *The Condition of Postmodernity* (Oxford: Basil Blackwell).

Hashim, I. and Thorsen, D. (2011) *Child Migration in Africa* (London: Zed Books).

Haugen, G. M. (2010) 'Children's perspectives on everyday experiences of shared residence: Time, emotions and agency dilemmas', *Children and Society*, 24, 112–122.

Head, E. (2005) 'The captive mother? The place of home in the lives of lone mothers', *Sociological Research Online*, 10, 9. Available at http://www.socresonline.org.uk/10/3/head.html, date accessed June 2012.

Heath, S., McGhee, D. and Trevena, P. (2011) 'Lost in transnationalism: Unraveling the conceptualisation of families and personal life through a transnational gaze', *Sociological Research Online*. Available at http://www.socresonline.org.uk/16/4/12.html, date accessed June 2012.

Hirschman, A. O. (1970) *Exit, Voice, and Loyalty: Responses to Decline in Firms, Organizations, and States* (Cambridge, MA: Harvard University Press).

Hodgson Burnett, F. (1911) *The Secret Garden* (London: Heinemann).

Holdsworth, C. (2006) ' "Don't you think you are missing out living at home?": Student experiences and residential transitions', *Sociological Review*, 54(3), 495–519.

Holdsworth, C. (2007) 'Intergenerational inter-dependencies: Mothers and daughters in comparative perspective', *Women's Studies International Forum*, 30(1), 59–69.

Holdsworth, C. (2009) ' "Going away to uni": Mobility, modernity and independence of English higher education students', *Environment and Planning A*, 41(8), 1849–1864.

Holdsworth, C. (2013) 'Subjects: Child' in P. Adey, D. Bissell, K. Hannam, P. Merrimen and M. Sheller (eds) *The Routledge Handbook of Mobilities* (London: Routledge), forthcoming.

Holdsworth, C. and Morgan, D. (2005) *Transitions In Context: Leaving Home, Independence and Adulthood* (Buckingham: Open University Press).

Holloway, S. and Valentine, G. (2000) 'Children's geographies and the new social studies of childhood' in S. Holloway and G. Valentine (eds) *Children's Geographies: Playing, Living, Learning* (London: Routledge), pp. 1–28.

Holmes, M. (2004) 'An equal distance? Individualisation, gender and intimacy in distance relationships', *The Sociological Review*, 52(2), 180–200.

Holmes, M. (2006) 'Love lives at a distance: distance relationships over the lifecourse', *Sociological Research Online*, 11, 3. Available at http://www.socresonline.org.uk/11/3/holmes.html, date accessed June 2012.

Holmes, M. (2010) 'The loves of others: Autoethnography and reflexivity in researching distance relationships', *Qualitative Sociology Review*, VI(2). Available at http://www.qualitativesociologyreview.org/ENG/archive_eng.php, date accessed June 2012.

Holt, L. and Costello, L. (2011) 'Beyond otherness: Exploring diverse spatialities and mobilities of childhood and youth populations', *Population, Space and Place*, 17(4), 299–303.

Hopkins, P. and Pain, R. (2007) 'Geographies of age: Thinking relationally', *Area*, 39(3), 287–294.

Horton, J. and Kraftl, P. (2008) 'Reflections on geographies of age', *Area*, 40(2), 284–288.

Hubbard, P. (2001) 'Sex zones: Intimacy, sexual citizenship and public space', *Sexualities*, 4(1), 51–71.

Hurdley, R. (2006) 'Dismantling mantelpieces: Narrating identities and materializing culture in the home', *Sociology*, 40(4), 717–733.

Iacovou, M. (2002) 'Regional differences in the transition to adulthood', *Annals of the American Academy of Political and Social Science*, 580(1), 40–69.

Illich, I. (1973) *Tools for Conviviality* (London: Calder and Boyers Ltd).

Imrie, R. (2004) 'Disability, embodiment and the meaning of home', *Housing Studies*, 19(5), 745–763.

Jamieson, L. (1998) *Intimacy* (Cambridge: Polity Press).

Jarvis, H. (1999) 'The tangled webs we weave: Household strategies to coordinate home and work', *Work, Employment and Society*, 13, 225–247.

Jarvis, H. (2005) 'Moving to London time: Household co-ordination and the infrastructure of everyday life', *Time and Society*, 14(1), 133–154.

Jarvis, H. (2011) 'Saving space, sharing time: Integrated infrastructures of daily life in cohousing', *Environment and Planning A*, 43, 560–577.

Jensen, A. -M. (2009) 'Mobile children: Small captives of large structures?', *Children and Society*, 23(2), 123–135.

Jones, G. (2009) *Youth* (Cambridge: Polity Press).

Jones, J. and Perrin, C. (2009) 'Third time lucky? The third child support reforms replace the Child Support Agency with the new C-MEC', *Journal of Social Welfare and Family Law*, 31(3), 333–342.

Kan, K. (2007) 'Residential mobility and social capital', *Journal of Urban Economics*, 61(3), 436–457.

Klein, A. (2011) 'Did children's education matter? Family migration as a mechanism of human capital investment: Evidence from nineteenth-century Bohemia', *Economic History Review*, 64(3), 730–764.

Kulu, H. (2008) 'Fertility and spatial mobility in the life course: Evidence from Austria', *Environment and Planning A*, 40(3), 632–652.

Kulu, H. and Billari, F. C. (2004) 'Multilevel analysis of internal migration in a transitional country: The case of Estonia', *Regional Studies*, 38(6), 679–696.

Kulu, H. and Boyle, P. (2010) 'Premarital cohabitation and divorce: Support for the "trial marriage" theory?', *Demographic Research*, 23, Article 31.

Langhamer, C. (2007) 'Love and courtship in mid-twentieth-century England', *The Historical Journal*, 50(1), 173–196.

Larsen, J., Axhausen, K. and Urry, J. (2006) *Mobilities, Networks and Geographies* (Aldershot: Ashgate).

Larsen, J., Urry, J. and Axhausen, K. W. (2007) 'Networks and tourism: Mobile social life', *Annals of Tourism Research*, 34(1), 244–262.

Laslett, T. P. R. (1965) *The World We Have Lost* (London: Routledge).

Laslett, T. P. R. (1983) *The World We Have Lost – Further Explored* (London).

Laurier, E. (2004) 'Doing office work on the motorway', *Theory, Culture and Society*, 21(4–5), 261–277.

Laurier, E., Lorimer, H., Brown, B., Jones, O., Juhlin, O., Noble, A., Perry, M., Pica, D., Sormani, P., Strebel, I., Swan, L., Taylor, A. S., Watts, L. and Weilenmann, A. (2008) 'Driving and "passengering": Notes on the ordinary organization of car travel', *Mobilities*, 3(1), 1–23.

Law, J. and Urry, J. (2004) 'Enacting the social', *Economy and Society*, 33(3), 390–410.

Law, R. (1999) 'Beyond "women and transport": Towards new geographies of gender and daily mobility', *Progress in Human Geography*, 23(4), 567–588.

Leonard, D. (1980) *Sex and Generation* (London: Tavistock).

Levin, I. (2004) 'Living apart together: A new family form', *Current Sociology*, 52(2), 223–240.

Levitt, P. (2001) *The Transnational Villagers* (Berkeley: University of California Press).

Löfgren, O. (1999) *On Holiday: A History of Vacationing* (Berkeley: University of California Press).

Louv, R. (2005) *Last Child in the Woods* (New York: Algonquin Books of Chapel Hill).

Lupton, D. (1998) *The Emotional Self* (London: Sage).

Macfarlane, A. (1978) *The Origins of English Individualism: The Family, Property and Social Transition* (Oxford: Blackwells).

Maddern, P. (2007) 'Moving households: Geographical mobility and serial monogamy in England, 1350–1500', *Parergon*, 24(2), 69–92.

Madigan, R., Munro, M. and Smith, S. J. (1990) 'Gender and the meaning of home', *International Journal of Urban and Regional Research*, 14, 625–647.

Mallett, S. (2004) 'Understanding home: A critical review of the literature', *Sociological Review*, 52(1), 62–89.

Malloch, M. S. and Burgess, C. (2011) 'Responding to young runaways: Problems of risk and responsibility', *Youth Justice*, 11, 61–76.

Mason, J. (1999) 'Living away from relatives: Kinship and geographical reasoning' in S. McRae (ed.) *Changing Britain: Families and Households in the 1990s* (Oxford: Oxford University Press), pp. 156–175.

Mason, J. (2004a) 'Managing kinship over long distances: The significance of "the visit" ', *Social Policy and Society*, 3(4), 421–429.

Mason, J. (2004b) 'Personal narratives, relational selves: Residential histories in the living and telling', *The Sociological Review*, 52(2), 162–179.

Massey, D. (1992) 'A place called home', *New Formations*, 17, 3–15.

Massey, D. (1993) 'Power-geometry and a progressive sense of place' in J. Bird, B. Curtis, T. Putnam, G. Robertson and L. Tickner (eds) *Mapping the Futures: Local Cultures, Global Change* (London: Routledge), pp. 59–69.

Matthews, H. and Limb, M. (1999) 'Defining an agenda for the geography of children: Review and prospect', *Progress in Human Geography*, 23(1), 61–90.

May, J. (1996) 'Globalization and the politics of place: Place and identity in an inner London neighbourhood', *Transactions of the Institute of British Geographers*, 21(1), 194–215.

McDowell, L. (1983) 'Towards an understanding of the gender division of urban space', *Environment and Planning D: Space and Society*, 1, 59–72.

McDowell, L. (2006) 'Reconfigurations of gender and class relations: Class differences, class condescension and the changing place of class relations', *Antipode*, 38(4), 825–850.

McDowell, L., Ward, K., Fagan, C., Perrons, D. and Ray, K. (2006) 'Connecting space and time: The significance of transformations in women's working lives and the structure of cities', *International Journal of Urban and Regional Research*, 30, 141–158.

McGlone, F., Park, A. and Roberts, C. (1999) 'Kinship and friendship: Attitudes and behaviour in Britain' in S. MacRae (ed.) *Changing Britain* (Oxford: OUP), pp. 141–155.

McHugh, K. E. (2000) 'Inside, outside, upside down, backward, forward, round and round: A case for ethnographic studies in migration', *Progress Human Geography*, 24, 71–89.

McHugh, K. E., Hogan, T. D. and Happel, S. K. (1995) 'Multiple residence and cyclical migration: A life course perspective', *Professional Geographer*, 47(3), 1–267.

McKay, D. (2007) ' "Sending dollars shows feeling": Emotions and economies in Filipino migration', *Mobilities*, 2(2), 175–194.

Meah, A., Hockey, J. and Robinson, V. (2008) 'What's sex got to do with it? A family-based investigation of growing up heterosexual during the twentieth century', *The Sociological Review*, 56(3), 454–473.

Merriman, P. (2004) 'Driving places: Marc Augé, non-places and the geographies of England's M1 motorway', *Theory, Culture, and Society*, 21(4–5), 145–167.

Michielin, K. and Mulder, C. (2008) 'Family events and the residential mobility of couples', *Environment and Planning A*, 40(11), 2770–2790.

Mikkelsen, M. R. and Christensen, P. (2009) 'Is children's independent mobility really independent? A study of children's mobility combining ethnography and GPS/mobile phone technologies', *Mobilities*, 4(1), 37–58.

Minnaert, L. for Tourism Flanders (2008) *Holidays are for Everyone: Research into the Effects and the Importance of Holidays for People living in Poverty* (Brussels: Tourism Flanders).

Morgan, D. H. J. (1996) *Family Connections* (Cambridge: Polity Press).

Morgan, D. H. J. (2008) 'Are community studies still "good to think with"?' in R. Edwards (ed.) *Researching Families and Communities: Social and Generational Change* (London: Routledge), pp. 24–40.

Morgan, D. H. J. (2011) *Rethinking Family Practices* (Basingstoke: Palgrave Macmillan).

Mulder, C. H. and Van Ham, M. (2005) 'Migration histories and occupational achievement', *Population, Space and Place*, 11(3), 173–186.

Mulder, C. H. and van der Meer, M. J. (2009) 'Geographical distances and support from family members', *Population, Space and Place*, 15(4), 381–399.

Ní Bhrolcháin, M., Chappell, R., Diamond, I. and Jameson, C. (2000) 'Parental divorce and outcomes for children: Evidence and interpretation', *European Sociological Review*, 16, 67–91.

Ní Laoire, C., Carpena-Méndez, F., Tyrrell, N. and White, A. (2010) 'Introduction: Childhood and migration – mobilities, homes and belongings',
Childhood, 17(2), 155–162.

Oakley, A. (1992) *Social Support and Motherhood* (Oxford: Blackwell Publishers).

Obrador, P. (2012) 'The place of the family in tourism research: Domesticity
and thick sociality by the pool', *Annals of Tourism Research*, 39(1), 401–420.

O'Connor, W. and Molloy, D. (2001) *'Hidden in Plain Sight': Homelessness
amongst Lesbian and Gay Youth* (London: National Centre for Social
Research).

Office for National Statistics (2011) *Families and Households in the UK, 2001 to
2010* (Cardiff: ONS).

Page Moch, L. (2003) *Moving Europeans: Migration in Western Europe since 1650*
(Bloomington: Indiana University Press).

Pahl, J. and Pahl, R. (1971) *Managers and Their Wives: A Study of Career and
Family Relationships in the Middle Class* (London: Allen Lane).

Pahl, R. (2008) 'Hertfordshire commuter villages: From geography to sociology', *International Journal of Social Research Methodology*, 11(2), 103–107.

Pahl, R. and Pahl, J. (1965–67) *Managers and Their Wives: A Study of Career
and Family Relationships in the Middle Class*. Qualidata Catalogue Number:
QDD/Pahl4 (Essex: Qualidata Archive, University of Essex).

Palmer, S. (2006) *Toxic Childhood: How the Modern World Is Damaging Our
Children and What We Can Do about It* (London: Orion).

Park, N. (2011) 'Military children and families: Strengths and challenges
during peace and war', *American Psychologist*, 66(1), 65–72.

Parkin, P. (1999) 'Mementoes as transitional objects in human displacement',
Journal of Material Culture, 4(3), 303–320.

Parreñas, R. (2005) 'Long distance intimacy: Class, gender and intergenerational relations between mothers and children in Filipino transnational
families', *Global Networks*, 5(4), 317–336.

Pearce, F. (2011) 'The end of the road for motormania', *New Scientist*. Available at http://www.newscientist.com/article/mg21128255.600-the-end-of-
the-road-for-motormania.html, date accessed June 2012.

Phillipson, C. (2007) 'The "elected" and the "excluded": Sociological perspectives on the experience of place and community in old age', *Ageing and
Society*, 27(3), 321–342.

Phillipson, C., Bernard, M., Phillips J. and Ogg, J. (2000) *The Family and Community Life of Older People: Social Networks and Social Support in Three Urban
Areas* (London: Routledge)

Pile, S. (2010) 'Emotions and affect in recent human geography', *Transactions
of the Institute of British Geographers*, 35, 5–20.

Pooley, C. G. and Turnbull, J. (2004) 'Migration from the parental home in
Britain since the eighteenth century' in F. van Poppel, M. Oris and J. Lee
(eds) *The Road to Independence* (Oxford: Peter Lang), pp. 375–402.

Pooley, C. G., Turnbull, J. and Adams, M. (2005) '...everywhere she went
I had to tag along beside her: Family life course, and everyday mobility in
England since the 1940s', *History of the Family*, 10, 119–136.

Porteous, J. D. (1976) 'Home: the territorial core', *Geographical Review*, 66, 383–390.

Power, A. (2007) *City Survivors: Bringing Up Children in Disadvantaged Neighbourhoods* (Bristol: Policy Press).

Probyn, E. (1996) *Outside Belongings* (London: Routledge).

Punch, S. (2002) 'Youth transitions and interdependent adult child relationships in rural Bolivia', *Journal of Rural Studies*, 18(2), 123–133.

Putnam, R. (2000) *Bowling Alone: The Collapse and Revival of American Community* (New York: Simon and Schuster).

Raval, V. V., Raval, P. H. and Raj, P. J. (2010) 'Damned if they flee, doomed if they don't: Narratives of runaway adolescent females from rural India', *Journal of Family Violence*, 25, 755–764.

Reher, D. S. (1998) 'Family ties in Western Europe: Persistent contrasts', *Population and Development Review*, 24, 203–234.

Reid Boyd, E. (2002) ' "Being there": Mothers who stay at home, gender and time', *Women's Studies International Forum*, 25(4), 463–470.

Relph, E. (1976) *Place and Placelessness* (London: Pion).

Ribbens McCarthy, J. (2012) 'The powerful relational language of "family": Togetherness, belonging and personhood', *The Sociological Review*, 60(1), 68–90.

Ribbens McCarthy, J. and Edwards, R. (2011) *Key Concepts in Family Studies* (London: Sage).

Roberts, K. (2007) 'Youth transitions and generations: a response to Wyn and Woodward', *Journal of Youth Studies*, 10(3), 263–269.

Roseneil, S. (2006) 'On not living with a partner: Unpicking coupledom and cohabitation', *Sociological Research Online*, 113. Available at http://www.socresonline.org.uk/11/3/roseneil.html.

Rossi, P. H. (1956) *Why Families Move* (Glencoe, IL: Free Press).

Ruggles, S. (2009) 'Reconsidering the North West European family system', *Population and Development Review*, 35(2), 249–273.

Ruggles, S. (2010) 'Stem Families and Joint Families in Comparative Historical Perspective', *Population and Development Review*, 36(3), 563–577.

Russell, J. (2012) 'Stalking – the terrifying crime the law may at last be taking seriously', *Guardian*, 6 March. Available at http://www.guardian.co.uk/commentisfree/2012/mar/06/stalking-crime-law-taking-seriously, date accessed May 2012.

Ryan, L. (2009) 'How women use family networks to facilitate migration: A comparative study of Irish and Polish women in Britain', *History of the Family*, 14(2), 217–231.

Rybczynski, W. (1986) *Home: A Short History of an Idea* (New York: Viking).

Satalkar, P. (2012) 'No "space" for love', paper presented at the Association of American Geographers Conference 2012, 'Geographies of Love' session, 26 February.

Saunders, P. (1990) *A Nation of Home Owners* (London: Unwin Hyman).

Savage, M. (2008) 'Histories, belongings, communities', *International Journal of Social Research Methodology*, 11(2), 151–162.

Savage, M., Bagnall, G. and Longhurst, B. (2005) *Globalization and Belonging* (London: Sage).

Schier, M. and Proske, A. (2010) One Child Two Homes *DJI Bulletin English Version* (Munich: Deutsches Jugendinstitu).

Schneider, N. F. and Collet, B. (eds) (2009) *Mobile Living across Europe: Volume II. Causes and Consequences of Job-Related Spatial Mobility in Cross-National Perspective* (Opladen: Barbara Budrich).

Schneider, N. F. and Meil, G. (eds) (2008) *Mobile Living across Europe: Volume I. Relevance and Diversity of Job-Related Spatial Mobility in Six European Countries* (Opladen: Barbara Budrich).

Schürer, K. (2004) 'Leaving home in England and Wales' in F. van Poppel, M. Oris and J. Lee (eds) *The Road to Independence* (Oxford: Peter Lang), pp. 33–84.

Settersten, R. and Ray, B. E. (2010) *Not Quite Adults* (New York: Random House).

Seymour, J. (2007) 'Treating the hotel like a home: The contribution of studying the single location home/workplace', *Sociology*, 41, 1097–1114.

Sheller, M. and Urry, J. (2000) 'The city and the car', *International Journal of Urban and Regional Research*, 24, 737–757.

Sheller, M. and Urry, J. (2006) 'The new mobilities paradigm', *Environment and Planning A*, 38, 207–226.

Shelton, N. and Grundy, E. (2000) 'Proximity of adult children to their parents in Great Britain', *International Journal of Population Geography*, 6, 181–196.

Sibley, D. (1995a) *Geographies of Exclusion: Society and Difference in the West* (London: Routledge).

Sibley, D. (1995b) 'Families and domestic routines: Constructing the boundaries of childhood' in S. Pile and N. Thrift (eds) *Mapping the Subject: Cultural Geographies of Transformation* (London: Routledge), pp. 114–131.

Sibley, D. and Lowe, G. (1992) 'Domestic space, modes of control and problem behaviour', *Geografiska Annaler*, 74B, 189–197.

Skeggs, B. (2004) *Class, Self and Culture* (London: Routledge).

Skelton, T. (2009) 'Children's geographies/geographies of children: Play, work, mobilities and migration', *Geography Compass*, 3(4), 1430–1448.

Skrbiş, Z. (2008) 'Transnational families: Theorising migration, emotions and belonging', *Journal of Intercultural Studies*, 29(3), 231–246.

Smart, C. (2007) *Personal Life* (Cambridge: Polity Press).

Smart, C. and Neale, B. (1999) *Family Fragments* (Cambridge: Polity Press).

Smith, D. (2011) 'Geographies of long-distance family migration:Moving to a "spatial turn" ', *Progress in Human Geography*, 35, 652–668.

Smith, R. M. (1981) 'Fertility, economy, and household formation in England over three centuries', *Population and Development Review*, 7(4), 595–622.

Sopher, D. (1979) 'The landscape of home: Myth, experience, social meaning' in W. Meinig (ed.) *The Interpretation of Ordinary Landscapes: Geographical Essays* (Oxford: OUP), pp. 129–149.

Stacey, J. (2011) *Unhitched: Love, Marriage, and Family Values from West Hollywood to Western China* (New York: New York University Press).

Stanko, E. (1985) *Intimate Intrusions: Women's Experiences of Male Violence* (London: Routledge and Kegan Paul).

Stanley, L. (1992) 'Changing households, changing work' in N. Abercrombie and A. Warde (eds) *Social Change in Contemporary Britain* (Cambridge: Polity), pp. 85–102.

Stillwell, J., Rees, P. and Duke-Williams, O. (1996) 'Migration between NUTS Level 2 regions in the United Kingdom' in P. Rees, J. Stillwell, A. Convey and M. Kupiszewski (eds) *Population Migration in the European Union* (London: Wiley), pp. 275–307.

Strand, S. and Demie, F. (2007) 'Pupil mobility, attainment and progress in secondary school', *Educational Studies*, 33(3), 313–331.

Svaşek, M. (2008) 'Who cares? Families and feelings in movement', *Journal of Intercultural Studies*, 29(3), 213–230.

Thompson, E. P. (1993) *Customs in Common* (London: Penguin).

Thompson, P. (1992) *The Edwardians: The Remaking of British Society* (London: Routledge).

Thompson, R. and Taylor, R. (2005) 'Between cosmopolitanism and the locals: Mobility as a resource in the transition to adulthood', *Young*, 13(4), 327–342.

Thornton, A. (2005) *Reading History Sideways: The Fallacy and Enduring Impact of the Developmental Paradigm on Family Life* (Chicago: University of Chicago Press).

Thrift, N. (2005) 'But malice aforethought: cities and the natural history of hatred', *Transactions of the Institute of British Geographers*, 30, 133–150.

Tuan, Y.-F. (1974) 'Space and place: Humanistic perspective', *Progress in Geography*, 6, 211–252.

Turkle, S. (2011) *Alone Together* (New York: Basic Books).

Urry, J. (2000) *Sociology beyond Societies: Mobilities for the Twenty-First Century* (London: Routledge).

Urry, J. (2002) 'Mobility and proximity', *Sociology*, 36(2), 255–274.

Urry, J. (2003) 'Social networks, travel and talk', *British Journal of Sociology*, 54 (2), 155–175.

Urry, J. (2007) *Mobilities* (Cambridge: Polity Press).

Uteng, T. P. and Cresswell, T. (eds) (2008) *Gendered Mobilities* (Aldershot: Ashgate).

Valentine, G. (1999) ' "Oh please, mum. Oh please, dad": negotiating children's spatial boundaries' in L. McKie, S. Bowlby and S. Gregory (eds) *Gender, Power and the Household* (Basingstoke: Palgrave Macmillan), pp. 137–154.

Valentine, G. and McKendrick, J. (1997) 'Children's outdoor play: Exploring parental concerns about children's safety and the changing nature of childhood', *Geoforum*, 28(2), 219–235.

van der Klis, M. and Karsten, L. (2009) 'The commuter family as a geographical adaptive strategy for the work-family balance', *Community, Work and Family*, 12(3), 339–354.

van der Klis, M. and. Mulder, C. H. (2008) 'Beyond the trailing spouse: The commuter partnership as an alternative to family migration', *Journal Housing and the Built Environment*, 23, 1–19.

Veness, A. (1992) 'Home and homelessness in the United States: Changing ideals and realities', *Environment and Planning D: Society and Space*, 10, 445–468.

Wade, A. and Smart, C. (2003) 'As fair as it can be? Childhood after divorce' in A. -M. Jensen and L. McKee (eds) *Children and the Changing Family* (London: Routledge), pp. 105–119.

Wagner, M. (1990) 'Education and migration' in K. U. Mayer and N. B. Tuma (eds) *Event History Analysis in Life Course Research* (Madison: The University of Wisconsin Press), pp. 129–145.

Wall, R. (1978) 'The age at leaving home', *Journal of Family History*, 3, 181–202.

Wall, R. (1987) 'Leaving home and the process of household formation in preindustrial England', *Continuity and Change*, 2, 77–101.

Walsh, M. (2009) 'Gender and travel: Mobilising new perspectives on the past' in G. Letherby and G. Reynolds (eds) *Gendered Journeys, Mobile Emotions* (Aldershot: Ashgate), pp. 5–18.

Warrington, M. (2001) ' "I must get out": the geographies of domestic violence', *Transactions of the Institute of British Geographers*, 26, 365–382.

Weilenmann, A. (2003) ' "I can't talk now, I'm in a fitting room": Availability and location in mobile phone conversations', *Environment and Planning A*, 35(9), 1589–1605.

Wenger, G. C. (1997) 'Social networks and the prediction of elderly people at risk', *Aging and Mental Health*, 1, 311–320.

Wheelock, J. and Jones, L. (2002) 'Grandparents are the next best thing': Informal childcare for working parents in urban Britain', *Journal Social Policy*, 31(3), 441–463.

White, A., Ní Laoire, C., Tyrrell, N. and Carpena-Méndez, F. (2011) 'Children's roles in transnational migration', *Journal of Ethnic and Migration Studies*, 37(8), 1159–1170.

Wilson, J. (1992) *The Suitcase Kid* (London: Random House).

Wittel, A. (2001) 'Towards a networked sociality', *Theory, Culture and Society*, 18(6), 51–76.

Wood, D. and Beck, R. J. (1994) *Home Rules* (Baltimore: Johns Hopkins University Press).

Woods, R. I. (1996) *The Demography of Victorian London* (Cambridge: Cambridge University Press).

Wyn, J. and Woodman, D. (2006) 'Generation, youth and social change in Australia', *Journal of Youth Research*, 9(5), 495–514.

Yeoh, B. S. A., Huang, B. and Lam, T. (2005) 'Transnationalizing the "Asian" family: imaginaries, intimacies and strategic intents', *Global Networks*, 5(4), 307–315.

Young, I. M. (200) *Inclusion and Democracy* (Oxford: Oxford University Press).

Young, M. and Willmott, P. (1957) *Family and Kinship in East London* (London: Routledge and Kegan Paul).

Author Index

Subject Index

Printed and bound in the United States of America